INCREDIBLE MACHINES

IAN GRAHAM

Silver Dolphin

San Diego, California

Silver Dolphin Books
An imprint of the Advantage
Publishers Group
10350 Barnes Canyon Road,
San Diego, CA 92121
www.silverdolphinbooks.com

ISBN-13: 978-1-59223-944-3
ISBN-10: 1-59223-944-7

Printed and bound in China
1 2 3 4 5   12 11 10 09 08

First published in the United States in 2007
by QEB Publishing Inc.
23062 La Cadena Drive, Laguna Hills, CA 92653
www.qeb-publishing.com

Written by Ian Graham
Produced by Calcium
Edited by Sarah Medina
Fold-out illustrations by Ian Naylor
Picture research by Maria Joannou

Publisher: Steve Evans
Creative Director: Zeta Davies
Senior Editor: Hannah Ray

Words in **bold** can be found in the glossary on page 232.

CONTENTS

More than 500 million cars drive along the world's roads today, and the number is growing all the time. Cars come in all shapes and sizes, from family cars and minivans to **sports cars**, off-road cars, and **supercars**. There are millions of motorcycles, too. Cars and motorcycles give people freedom to travel, but there are so many vehicles now that traffic jams often cause delays at busy times.

Building cars

Most cars are made from steel parts **welded** together. In a modern car factory, robots do this work. They also move parts into position to be fitted to cars. People still do all the trickier work needed to finish off each vehicle, such as putting in the seats.

▼ Robots build cars on a factory production line.

robot

ENGINE POWER

Most cars and motorcycles are driven by engines that burn a fuel such as gasoline. **The gasoline is sprayed into a tube-shaped** cylinder. **A spark sets the** fuel **on fire. The air heats up and** expands, **which pushes a tight-fitting** piston **down the cylinder. Pistons moving like this in four or more cylinders provide the force to turn the car or motorcycle's wheels.**

The **power** to drive a car comes ➤ from its engine. The driver makes the engine go faster by pressing a pedal.

FACT!
By the year 2050, there could be nearly a **billion** cars on the world's roads.

▲ Road transportation is essential in the modern world.

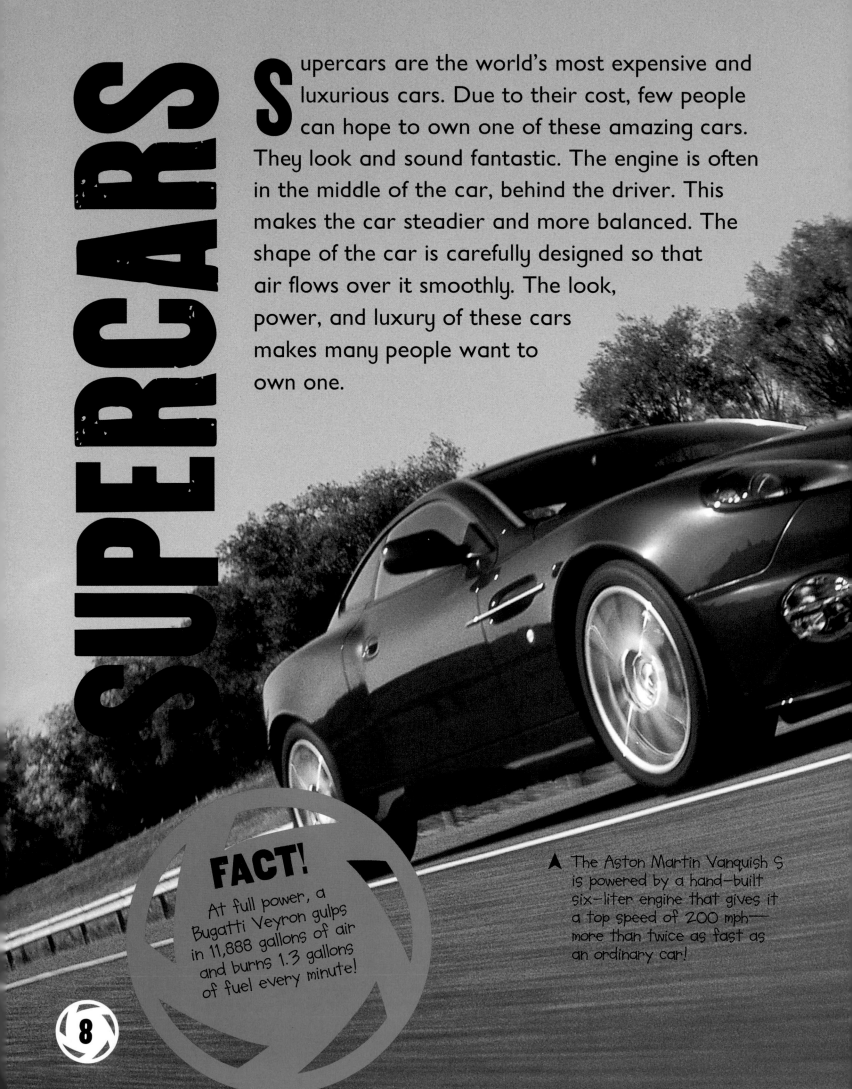

SUPERCARS

Supercars are the world's most expensive and luxurious cars. Due to their cost, few people can hope to own one of these amazing cars. They look and sound fantastic. The engine is often in the middle of the car, behind the driver. This makes the car steadier and more balanced. The shape of the car is carefully designed so that air flows over it smoothly. The look, power, and luxury of these cars makes many people want to own one.

FACT!

At full power, a Bugatti Veyron gulps in 11,888 gallons of air and burns 1.3 gallons of fuel every minute!

▲ The Aston Martin Vanquish S is powered by a hand-built six-liter engine that gives it a top speed of 200 mph— more than twice as fast as an ordinary car!

rear wing

Bugatti Veyron

Everything about the Bugatti Veyron is mind-boggling. It has a huge engine that is actually two normal car engines side-by-side. They give the Veyron a top speed of 250 mph. At high speeds, a wing rises up at the back of the car to hold it steady on the road.

▲ The Bugatti Veyron's beautiful body is made from a material called **carbon fiber**.

PORSCHE'S SUPERCAR

The Porsche Carrera GT goes from zero to 62 mph in under four seconds. Most cars take two or three times longer than this. The power for this great performance is supplied by a 605-horsepower engine behind the driver, which is three or four times more powerful than the engine in a family car.

▲ Only a few hundred Porsche Carrera GT supercars are built every year.

SPORTS CARS

Some people enjoy driving so much that they want a car that is lots of fun to drive. Sports cars are small and fast. They do not have much space for carrying luggage, and they usually have just two seats. This makes them shorter than other cars. They are lighter and more **maneuverable**, so they are fun to drive. Some sports cars have a top that folds down for open-top driving in good weather.

▲ The open-top Audi R8 is one of the most successful racing sports cars.

SPORTS RACERS

There are motor races especially for sports cars. Some of the cars that take part are more powerful racing versions of ordinary sports cars. Others are specially designed racing sports cars, such as the Audi R8, which can reach 200 mph or more.

Corvette

The first Chevrolet Corvette sports car was built more than 50 years ago, in 1953. It was an instant success. It has been updated, or redesigned, regularly since then. The latest Corvette has a six-liter, 400-horsepower engine. This is one of the biggest engines in any sports car.

The most powerful sports cars, ▶ such as the Chevrolet Corvette, are sometimes called muscle cars.

▲ The world-famous sports car race held at Le Mans in France goes on for 24 hours—all day and all night!

OFF-ROAD

Most cars are designed for normal roads. They drive well on dry and wet roads, and they can also cope with firm earth and grass. However, they get stuck easily in soft or muddy ground, which makes their wheels spin and sink. Off-road cars are designed especially for these conditions. There is more space between the ground and the bottom of the car so they can bump over uneven, rocky ground without getting damaged underneath. They also have special tires to give them more grip.

Power plus

A normal car engine usually drives just the two front wheels or the two back wheels of the car. This two-wheel drive is good for roads, but it does not grip soft ground well. Off-road cars are also called 4x4s (four-by-fours) or **four-wheel drives** because the engine drives all four wheels to give extra grip.

A 4x4 off-road car has twice ➤ as much grip as other cars.

EXTRA WHEELS

One way to get better grip on wet or loose ground is to reduce the car's weight and to add more wheels. Some extreme off-roaders have six—or even eight—wheels. They are not the fastest or best-looking vehicles, but they leave other cars far behind in the worst ground conditions.

▲ A car with lots of wheels can grip soft ground better.

▲ Off-road cars make short work of wet or muddy ground.

FACT!
The World War II U.S. Jeep became one of the most famous 4x4 vehicles ever.

PEDAL POWER

Bicycles have existed for about 200 years. Today, cars and motorcycles are faster, but pedal-powered bikes are more popular than ever. They are simple machines that work well and they can be repaired easily. There is no engine, so they do not need to fill up with fuel to work—they are human-powered vehicles (HPVs). The pedals and **gears** on a bike make them easier to ride. Changing gear can make it easier to go faster or cycle uphill. Some bikes have as many as 30 gears.

FACT!

The first mountain bikes were made in the 1970s in the United States.

CARBON RACERS

The bikes ridden by cyclists in the Olympic Games look different from other bikes. The frame is made from lightweight carbon fiber instead of steel. The wheels have broad blades instead of wire spokes, or they may be even more streamlined solid disks. These differences make the bikes much faster.

solid disk wheel

▲ Olympic racing bikes are lighter and more streamlined than other bikes.

Mountain bikes

Mountain bikes are designed for riding on rough tracks. They are also called all-terrain bikes. They have a stronger frame and wheels than other bikes, and can bump along rocky ground without bending or breaking. Their fat, knobbly tires give better grip on loose ground.

◄ BMX bikes are small and strong for racing on hilly dirt tracks or for freestyle stunt riding.

▲ Mountain bikes have to be strongly built for rough riding.

RESCUE

Police and medical services use cars and bikes for emergency rescue work. A car can carry people and equipment, but a motorcycle is faster. An experienced **paramedic** on a fast motorcycle can give life-saving help before an ambulance arrives. A police motorcyclist can speed to a trouble spot, even on roads blocked by traffic jams. Bicycles are useful for this work, too. Police officers and paramedics can cover ground faster on bicycles than they can on foot.

The U.S. car company Dodge makes ➤ this special police version of its Charger car for police forces.

POLICE BIKES

Police officers on motorcycles are a common sight. Police motorcycles can squeeze between lines of traffic that hold up police cars. The bikes are specially adapted for police work. They carry extra equipment. In addition to flashing lights and a siren, they can be fitted with radar and video equipment to check on other road users.

▲ The Harley-Davidson police motorcycle is a favorite with many U.S. police forces.

Pedal force

Police officers and paramedics on mountain bikes can get around obstructions and through crowds quickly. They can even **patrol** inside big buildings, such as stations and airport terminals, where cars and motorcycles cannot go. They keep in touch with other officers by radio.

▲ Officers on bikes can answer nearby calls quickly.

FACT!

Sea-Tac Airport in Seattle, Washington, is patrolled by 20 police officers on mountain bikes.

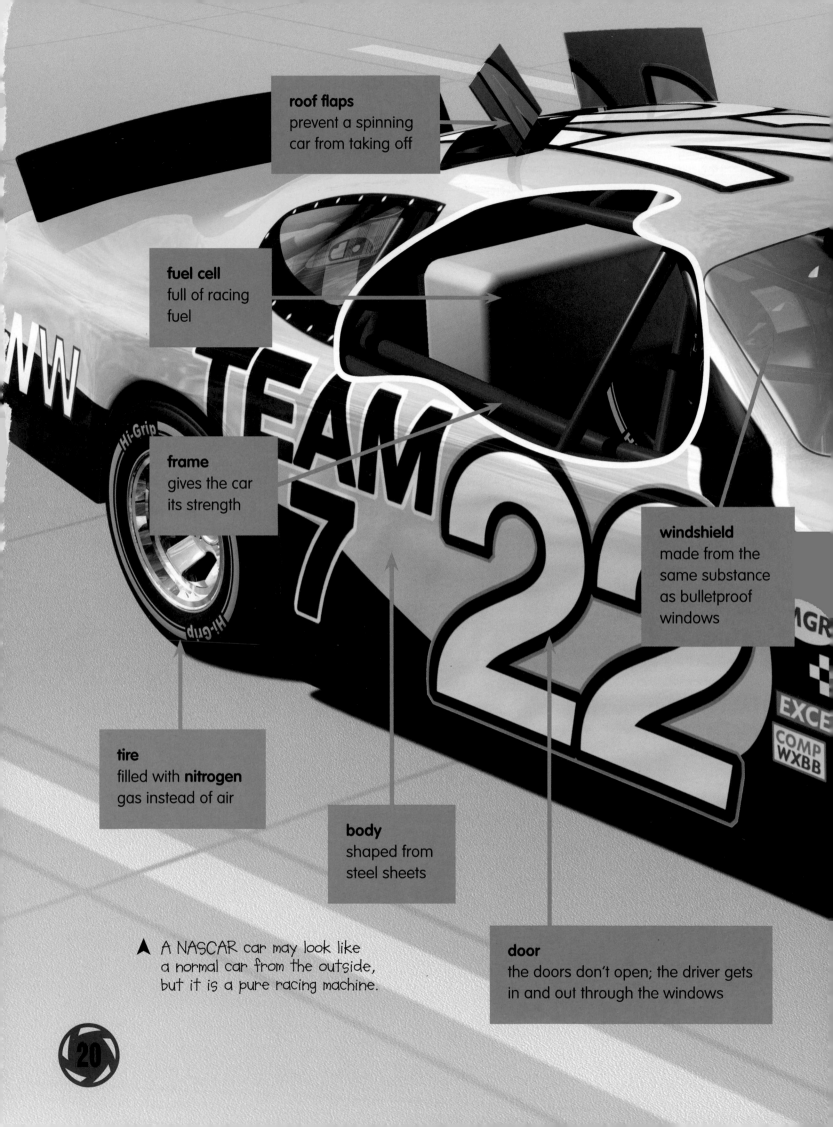

roof flaps
prevent a spinning
car from taking off

fuel cell
full of racing
fuel

frame
gives the car
its strength

windshield
made from the
same substance
as bulletproof
windows

tire
filled with **nitrogen**
gas instead of air

body
shaped from
steel sheets

door
the doors don't open; the driver gets
in and out through the windows

▲ A NASCAR car may look like
a normal car from the outside,
but it is a pure racing machine.

20

NASCAR

NASCAR racing is the most popular motor sport in the United States, with more than 75 million fans. NASCAR stands for the National Association for Stock Car Auto Racing. It started in the 1940s with races between stock, or ordinary, cars. NASCAR cars look a little like ordinary cars, but they are all custom-built especially for racing. They do not have the modern computers or **aerodynamic** bodies that are used in other motor sports, but they have a lot of power. Most NASCAR races are held on oval tracks with sharp turns that make for very exciting races.

Under the hood

NASCAR cars are powered by a 5.87-liter engine. It works exactly like a big ordinary car engine, but it is specially built to produce the maximum power for racing. It is more than twice as powerful as an ordinary car engine of the same size.

◄ NASCAR cars can reach speeds of more than 200 mph.

ROOF FLAPS

If a NASCAR race car spins around and slides backward along the track, it could take off like a plane! Flaps on the roof prevent this from happening. If a car spins, the flaps pop up. This means the car does not take the shape of a wing, so it does not take off into the air.

Rooftop flaps prevent cars from ▲ taking off and flying through the air.

RACING CARS

Racing cars combine great power, light weight, and a streamlined shape. Some racing cars are based on ordinary cars, but they have more powerful engines and stronger bodies for racing. Others, such as **IndyCars**, are specially designed for racing. IndyCars and **Formula 1** cars are **single-seaters**. The car's long, slim body is so low down between the wheels that the driver has to lie on his back to drive the vehicle.

Single-seaters

There is no room for the engine at the front of a single-seat racing car, so it sits behind the driver. The car has wings on its nose and tail to help it go around corners faster. As the wings slice through the air, they suck the car downward, pressing the tires down harder. This is called **downforce**.

rear wing

nose wing

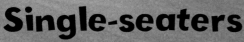
Wings make IndyCars ➤ faster through turns.

CHEWY TIRES

A racing car's tires heat up during a race. They can get as hot as boiling water! At that temperature, the rubber is like tar or chewing gum. It sticks to the road better, but it soon starts to break up. That is why cars have to have new wheels fitted during a race.

▲ A racing car's tires may last only 100 miles before they have to be changed.

▼ IndyCars are nearly four times as powerful as ordinary cars.

FACT!

At top speed, an IndyCar's front wheels spin more than 40 times every second!

At the wheel

A NASCAR car driver sits in a wraparound seat that gives extra protection in case of a crash. The driver is held in the seat by a special harness with five extra-strong seat belts. The side windows are covered with nets to keep parts of the car from flying into the driver during a crash.

▲ A driver sits strapped into his seat inside a strong steel cage before a NASCAR race.

Safety first

NASCAR cars are designed to protect the driver if they should crash. The nose and tail of the car are made weaker than the middle. They soak up the impact of a crash by crumpling, while the driver sits inside a superstrong steel cage.

The nose of a NASCAR ▲ racing car is designed to crumple in a crash.

headlights
not real—just for show!

FACT!
A good NASCAR team can refuel a car and change all of its wheels in less than 14 seconds!

22

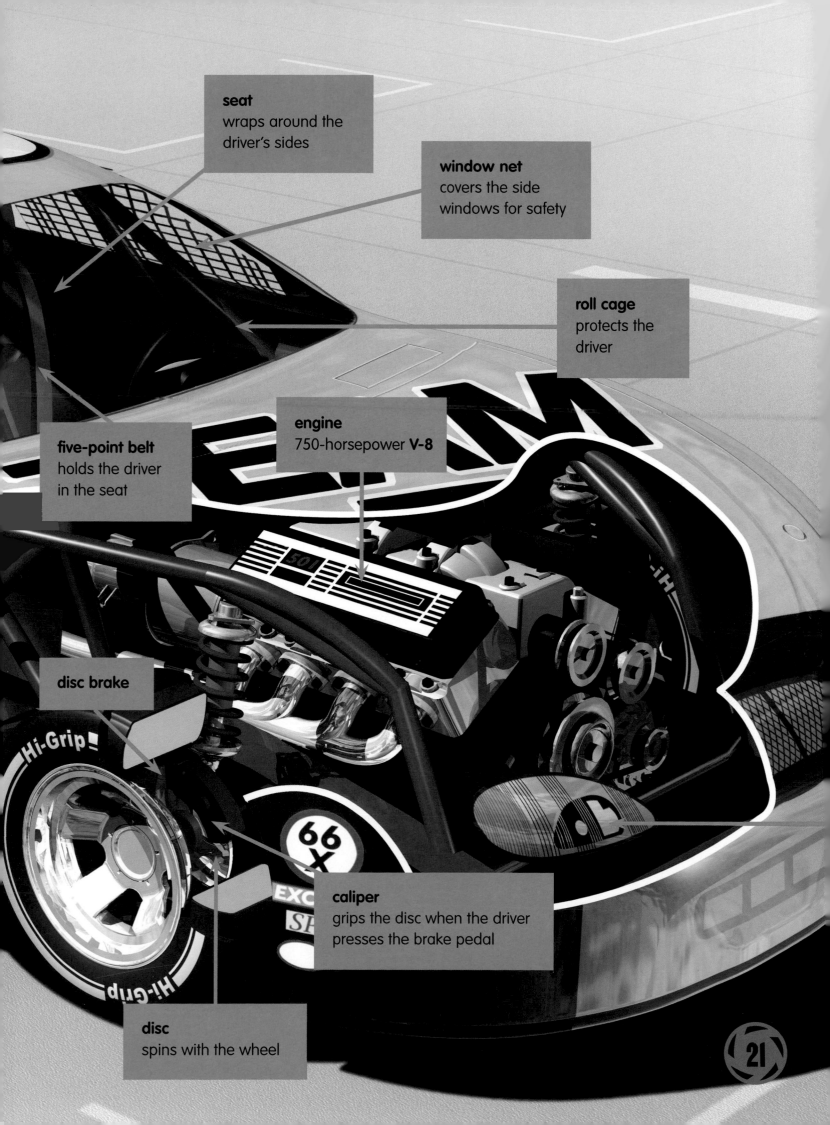

seat
wraps around the
driver's sides

window net
covers the side
windows for safety

roll cage
protects the
driver

engine
750-horsepower **V-8**

five-point belt
holds the driver
in the seat

disc brake

caliper
grips the disc when the driver
presses the brake pedal

disc
spins with the wheel

Hi-Grip

66
X

SUPERPOWER

Dragsters are the fastest and most powerful racing cars. They do not race around tracks like other racing cars. They are designed to do one simple thing—to go as fast as possible in a straight line! The cars race two at a time along a straight track called a **drag strip**. There are different classes of dragsters with their own rules. The long, thin Top Fuel dragsters are the fastest, and they can reach speeds of 330 mph.

In the cockpit

The driver's seat of a Top Fuel dragster is a scary place to be. The driver is strapped tightly into a seat inside a steel cage. He wears a fireproof suit and crash helmet.

Smoke and flames ➤ are a normal part of drag races.

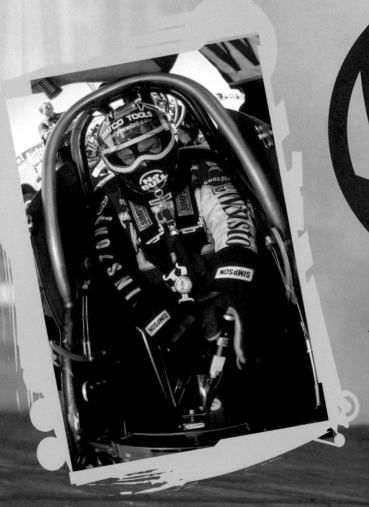

FACT!
A Top Fuel dragster race may last as little as five seconds!

◄ A Top Fuel dragster driver sits in a cramped **cockpit** and waits for the signal to go.

rear wing

engine air
intakes

engine

wheelie
bar

small front
wheels

DRAG BIKES

Cars are not the only drag racers. There are drag bikes, too. A drag bike's big back wheel turns with such a great force that it can flip the whole bike over on its back. A long bar trailing behind the bike stops this.

▼ A drag bike rider leans forward on the bike to make a more streamlined shape.

DIRT DEVILS

Imagine driving at 100 mph—faster than in the fast lane of a highway—on slippery roads or in fog. It sounds dangerous, but this is exactly how **rally** cars are driven. Rally drivers set off one by one, and they drive as fast as they can to set the fastest time in each race, or **stage**. They do this on closed roads through forests, countryside, or even mountains! Rally cars look like ordinary cars, but they are specially built for rallying.

World rally cars

The cars that take part in the biggest rally, the World Rally Championship, have a two-liter engine and are three times more powerful than a normal car. Their top speed is about 125 mph.

▼ A team of mechanics may have only a few minutes to repair a rally car between stages, no matter what's wrong!

INSIDE THE CAR

The car's crew sits inside a strong cage, which keeps the roof from being flattened if the car turns over. The driver concentrates on driving. The navigator looks at a map and some notes, and warns the driver about what is coming up ahead—for example, a sharp turn or a rise or dip in the road.

◄ Rally crews are strapped tightly into their seats by extra-strong seat belts called harnesses.

FACT!
It costs thousands of dollars to produce a World Rally Championship car!

▲ Rally drivers do not slow down over bumps!

SUN CARS

The most extraordinary racing cars are powered by nothing more than sunlight! Sunlight power is also called **solar power**. A solar-powered car is covered with special parts called solar cells that change sunlight into electricity. The electricity runs an electric motor that drives the wheels. The most famous race for solar-powered cars is the World Solar Challenge in Australia. Teams bring cars from all over the world to take part.

FACT!

World Solar Challenge cars race 1,864 miles across Australia, from Darwin to Adelaide.

Solar-powered racing cars can drive along at more than 62 mph. ➤

solar cells

streamlined wheels

Nuna 3

The 2005 World Solar Challenge race was won by a car from the Netherlands called Nuna 3. Nuna 3 is a three-wheeled car. The tiny electric motor that drives it is inside the rear wheel. The driver sees the road ahead through a plastic bubble on top of the car.

▲ Every part of Nuna 3 is carefully shaped to reduce **air resistance** that would slow it down.

Aurora made the ➤ longest–ever **solar car** journey by traveling 8,111 miles around Australia in 24 days.

AURORA

Aurora is an Australian solar racing car. It won the World Solar Challenge race in 1999 and came in second four times. The car stands only 37 inches high. The driver has to lie down inside its body.

MOTORCYCLES

People have been building motorcycles for more than 120 years. Today, there are all sorts of different motorcycles. There are big, comfortable cruisers for touring, commuter cycles for short city journeys, specially designed sports cycles, lightweight trail cycles, and fast racing cycles. All motorcycles have the same basic layout, because it works well. The engine sits under the seat in the middle of a strong frame called the chassis. The engine usually drives the back wheel by means of a chain.

▲ Motocross riders often fly through the air as they reach the tops of hills.

RACING BIKES

Superbike, MotoGP, and Motocross are all types of motorcycle racing. Superbikes are racing versions of ordinary road motorcycles. MotoGP cycles are designed just for racing. Superbikes and MotoGP races are held on road tracks. Motocross races are held on hilly dirt tracks. Supercross is a type of Motocross held on specially built indoor dirt tracks.

Touring cycles

Touring cycles are built for long journeys. Their big engines can purr along the roads for hours. They have carriers for luggage, and the upright riding position is comfortable. Some touring cycles even have a built-in sound system to feed music into the rider's helmet!

The Honda Gold Wing is ▲ a popular touring cycle.

FACT!

The Suzuki Hayabusa is the fastest superbike, with a top speed of 195 mph.

▲ A MotoGP rider leans his bike over to make a tight turn.

RECORD BREAKERS

The cars and motorcycles that set speed and distance records have two things in common. They have powerful engines to boost them to the highest possible speed. They also look like planes or rockets, because these are the best shapes to reduce air resistance. The world's fastest car goes faster than an **airplane**, but the team of designers and engineers who built it had to make sure it would not take off like a plane!

jet engine

Easy record

The world's fastest motorcycle is called Easyriders. The rider does not sit on top of it like a normal motorcycle. Instead, he sits inside its slim body along with two powerful engines. In 1990, Dave Campos set a new world record by taking Easyriders up to 322 mph.

The rocket-shaped motorcycles that set speed records are called **streamliners**. ➤

32

FASTER THAN SOUND

The record-breaking Thrust SSC car has two engines, but they are not like other car engines. They are jet engines! In 1997, UK Royal Air Force pilot Andy Green set a new speed record of 762 mph in the Thrust SSC—faster than the speed of sound.

▲ The Thrust SSC is the first supersonic car.

▲ The Thrust SSC is the fastest car in the world.

FACT!
The Thrust SSC set the first supersonic speed record in the Black Rock Desert in Nevada.

FUTURE

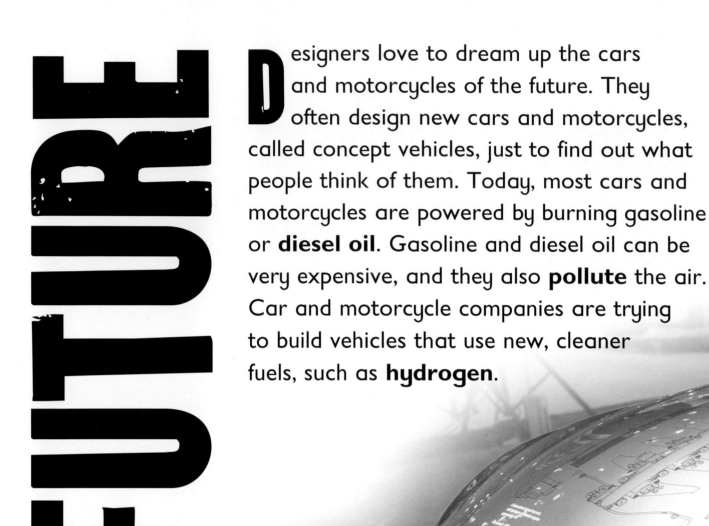

Designers love to dream up the cars and motorcycles of the future. They often design new cars and motorcycles, called concept vehicles, just to find out what people think of them. Today, most cars and motorcycles are powered by burning gasoline or **diesel oil**. Gasoline and diesel oil can be very expensive, and they also **pollute** the air. Car and motorcycle companies are trying to build vehicles that use new, cleaner fuels, such as **hydrogen**.

▲ Future motorcycles could have a completely different shape.

FUTURE BIKES

Designers are always trying new shapes and new materials for future vehicles. Motorcycles have always had to be built around a big gasoline engine. By getting rid of the engine and using fuel cells instead, future motorcycles could be made in all sorts of new shapes.

◀ Fuel-cell cars such as this Honda FCX Hydrogen Fuel Concept Car could be on the roads by 2010.

Hydrogen power

Hydrogen is a clean fuel. When it burns in an engine, it produces water. Hydrogen can also be used in a different way, without burning it. It can make electricity in a fuel cell. Electricity from a fuel cell powers an electric motor that drives the car's wheels. Future cars may be powered by fuel cells.

FACT!

Hydrogen-powered fuel cells make electricity in the space shuttle.

▲ The BMW HR2 is a futuristic hydrogen-powered racing car that holds nine speed records.

ON THE RAILS

Railway lines crisscross the world. They spread out from major cities like huge steel spiderwebs. Every day, trains thunder along the tracks, carrying millions of workers into towns and cities. They take people away on vacation and move **billions** of tons of goods and materials. The latest **high-speed** passenger trains carry hundreds of people in comfortable **cars**. These trains are almost as fast as a small plane. The trains that do all these jobs are very powerful machines.

▲ One train can carry as many people as hundreds of cars.

Rail or road?

Railways are a good way to move people and materials. A modern high-speed railway line can carry more traffic than a six-lane highway, but takes up much less space. Trains create far less **air pollution** than a highway full of traffic, so they are also kinder to the **environment**.

MOVING MOUNTAINS

Freight **trains** transport the goods and materials that modern life depends on. They move tons of earth and rock, and transport cars and other goods made in factories. They also move oil and other **fuels** needed to run all sorts of vehicles and machines, and deliver coal to power stations to provide the electricity we need.

▲ Two freight trains pull **wagons** full of coal through Wyoming.

2000

Amtrak

FACT!
The world's first locomotive was built by Richard Trevithick in 1804.

▲ After planes, high-speed passenger trains are the fastest way to travel!

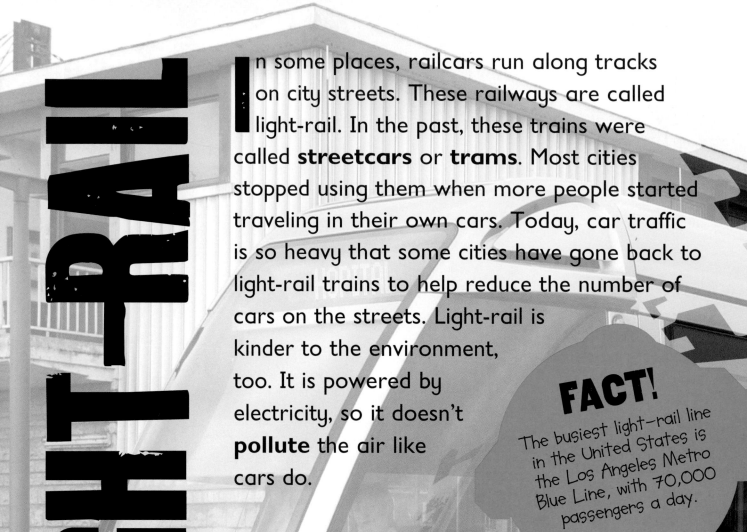

LIGHT-RAIL

In some places, railcars run along tracks on city streets. These railways are called light-rail. In the past, these trains were called **streetcars** or **trams**. Most cities stopped using them when more people started traveling in their own cars. Today, car traffic is so heavy that some cities have gone back to light-rail trains to help reduce the number of cars on the streets. Light-rail is kinder to the environment, too. It is powered by electricity, so it doesn't **pollute** the air like cars do.

FACT!

The busiest light-rail line in the United States is the Los Angeles Metro Blue Line, with 70,000 passengers a day.

Powering up

Most light-rail cars pick up the electric current they need from wires hanging over the road. A frame on top of the railcars pushes up against the wires. As the railcars move, the frame slides along the wires. The electric current then flows down through the frame into the vehicle's electric motors.

▲ Light-rail cars can be powered from cables above the car or by an electric rail in the road.

▼ About 45,000 people a day travel on the light-rail line in Orléans, France.

JULES VERNE

54

FLEXIBLE CARS

Light-rail cars have to run along existing streets, traveling alongside all the other traffic. The longer a light-rail train is, the more passengers it can carry, but if it is too long, it cannot make sharp turns. The solution is to make a light-rail train that bends in the middle!

▲ Light-rail trains bend where the cars connect to each other.

39

GOING UNDERGROUND

Underground railways avoid the traffic on busy city streets because the trains travel in tunnels dug under the city. Gasoline or **diesel engines** would fill the stations with dangerous **fumes**, so trains that run underground are powered by electric motors. Underground railways are also called **subways** or **metros**. Some cities have fast city transport systems called **mass transit** or **rapid transit** systems. These often use underground railways, as well as railways on, or even high above, the ground.

➤ The New York City subway uses enough electric power to provide light for a city of nearly 300,000 people.

▲ Line 14 in the Paris Metro has automatic trains that run without drivers.

Trains without drivers

The most modern underground railways have automatic trains—there are no drivers! The trains automatically stay a safe distance from the train in front and constantly report where they are to a control room. In France, one of the Paris Metro's lines is fully automatic. The world's biggest automatic underground railway is being built in Singapore.

SUPERSUBWAY

The New York City subway is the biggest underground railway in the world. When it opened in 1904, there were 28 stations. Today, there are 468! More than 6,000 cars run on the subway network. They are powered by electricity from a third rail running alongside the tracks.

SPECIALS

Trains consist of locomotives and cars. Most trains are made in large numbers, and they all look much the same as each other. However, there are a few trains that stand out from the others. The Orient Express and the Trans-Siberian Express are world-famous passenger trains. Some other trains do very unusual jobs! There are telescopes that move around on railway tracks and, in Russia, rockets are delivered to the **launch pad** by rail.

The Trans–Siberian Express goes ➤ from Moscow to Vladivostok on Russia's east coast.

▲ Orient Express cars date from the 1920s and 1930s.

THE ORIENT EXPRESS

The Orient Express has carried passengers across Europe since 1883. Orient means "east." Originally, the train traveled from Paris, France, eastward to Istanbul, Turkey. Today, the Orient Express goes from London or Paris to Venice, Italy. Some people think that the Orient Express is the most luxurious way to travel by rail.

A Soyuz rocket arrives at its ➤
Russian launch pad by rail.

Rocket rail

Rocket parts arrive at the Baikonur Cosmodrome (space center) in Russia by air. Then they are loaded onto wagons on a track beside the runway. The track leads to the building where the rockets are built. Each completed rocket is loaded onto a railcar so that it can be taken out to the launch pad.

FACT!

The Trans-Siberian Express takes about seven days to complete its 5,773-mile journey.

43

FREIGHT

Enormous amounts of goods and materials, known as freight, are sent by rail. In the United States, more than 2 billion tons of freight cross the country by rail every year. The heaviest freight trains carry coal away from mines in wagons. The wagons are pulled by very powerful locomotives. Three, four, or even more locomotives are often hooked together to pull freight trains that have more than a hundred wagons.

diesel locomotive

FACT!
The heaviest freight train pulled 100,935 tons and was more than 4.5 miles long!

➤ Rail is the best way to carry heavy materials over long distances.

Container freight

Many goods are transported in metal boxes that are all the same size. They are called freight or shipping containers. They can be lifted off a truck and lowered onto a wagon very quickly by specially built cranes. The cranes themselves often move on rails, too.

▲ Freight containers make it quicker to load and unload freight trains.

◀ Satellites keep track of freight trains in remote parts of North America, South Africa, and Australia.

freight wagon

KEEPING TRACK

For safety reasons, freight managers like to know exactly where freight is during its journey. Freight trains often have electronic boxes called transponders. They send information to receivers beside the track. The receivers then send the information on to the freight managers. Satellites **are used to track trains in remote areas.**

STEAM

The first trains were powered by steam engines. In most places, steam trains disappeared long ago. They were replaced by diesel and electric trains. Old steam trains are still used in a few places. In parts of China, India, Africa, and South America, steam trains haul coal, wood, and other raw materials.

Some steam trains have been **restored** so that people can ride in them today.

▲ You can see old steam trains on display at museums and history parks, like this one in Yuma, Arizona.

Steam power

A steam train works by burning coal or wood to heat water. When the water gets very hot, it changes into steam. Steam takes up more space than water. The force of the steam **expanding** in a small space pushes **pistons** in and out of **cylinders**. The powerful movements of these pistons turn the train's wheels.

▲ The power to move a huge steam train comes from hot water!

▼ A miniature steam train may be small, but it is still powerful enough to pull a long line of passenger cars.

driver's **cab**

2521

TINY TRAINS

In some places, you can go for a ride in a steam train that is much smaller than an ordinary train. Some of these miniature trains are so small that the driver has to sit on top! Even so, they work just like full-size steam trains.

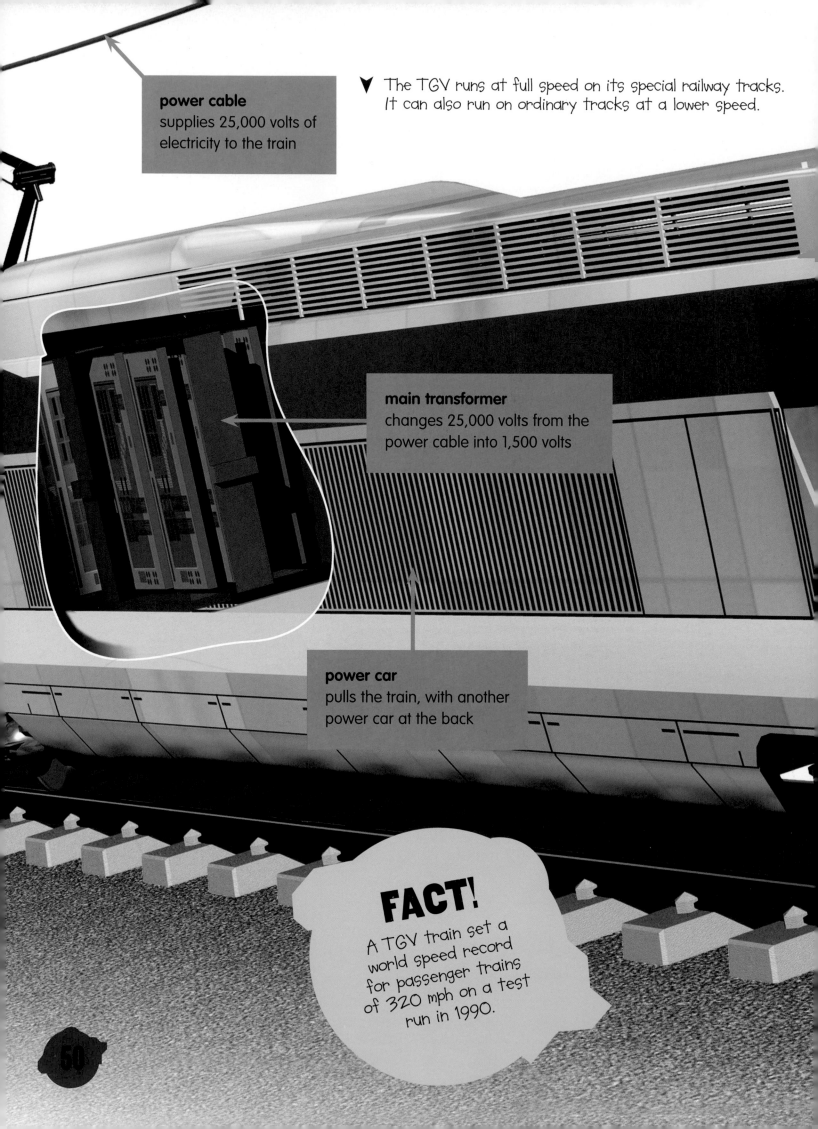

power cable
supplies 25,000 volts of electricity to the train

▼ The TGV runs at full speed on its special railway tracks. It can also run on ordinary tracks at a lower speed.

main transformer
changes 25,000 volts from the power cable into 1,500 volts

power car
pulls the train, with another power car at the back

FACT!

A TGV train set a world speed record for passenger trains of 320 mph on a test run in 1990.

TGV

The TGV is France's high-speed passenger train. TGV stands for Train à Grande Vitesse, which means "high-speed train." The TGV started carrying passengers in 1981. TGVs normally travel at up to 196 mph, but they have gone a lot faster in special test runs. In fact, a TGV holds the world speed record for the fastest passenger train. TGV trains are very popular with travelers in France. Many people prefer to travel by TGV rather than by plane.

pantograph
collects electricity from an overhead cable

Going electric

When the first TGV was built in the 1970s, it was powered by a **jet engine**. Then the fuel that the engine burned became too expensive. Because of this, the TGV was changed to make it an electric train. An overhead power cable now supplies it with 25,000 **volts** of electricity.

The TGV runs on electricity from overhead cables. ▶

HIGH SPEED

High-speed trains can carry passengers at more than 124 mph! Most of them are powered by electricity from wires hanging above the track. Because the train does not have big, heavy tanks of fuel, it can go faster. The shape of a high-speed train is important. The Japanese Shinkansen, the French TGV, and the German ICE high-speed trains are designed to go very fast. They all have a sloping front and a smooth body to help them slip through the air.

streamlined body

The Japanese Shinkansen ▲ train was called the **Bullet Train** when it first came out, due to its shape and speed.

FACT!
Japanese Shinkansen trains stop automatically if they are shaken by an earthquake!

Acela Express

The fastest train in the United States is the Acela Express. It has been running the 398 miles between Washington, D.C., and Boston since 2000. On the fastest part of the track, it reaches 149 mph.

◄ Acela Express trains have four passenger cars between two locomotives.

ICE-COOL TRAIN

ICE stands for Inter-City Express. The ICE trains are high-speed trains made in Germany. They started running in 1991. The latest ICE trains carry passengers at up to 186 mph. In tests, they have gone faster than 249 mph—nearly four times faster than cars on a highway!

▲ ICE trains run fastest on their own special tracks. They run at normal speeds on ordinary tracks.

53

STOP AND GO

The movements of trains are usually controlled by signals beside the track. However, the TGV goes so fast that the driver would not have time to see signals flashing past outside. Instead, signal information is sent along the tracks. It is picked up by the train and the driver sees the signals on his instrument panel.

Traffic signals are sent straight into the driver's cab. ▲

automatic coupler connects the power car to other vehicles, if necessary

Power cars

Each TGV train has two locomotives, which are also called **power cars**. There is one at the front of the train and one at the back. They are packed full of electronic equipment, including a transformer. The transformer changes the electric current from the overhead power cable into the right form of electricity to run the train's electric motors.

▼ A TGV train has two power cars, with eight or ten cars in between them.

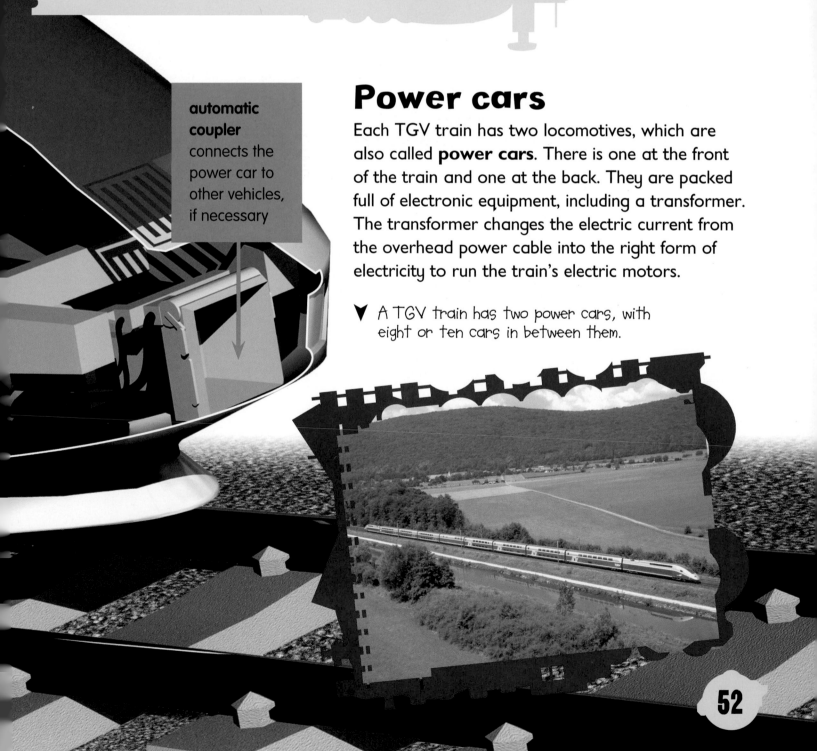

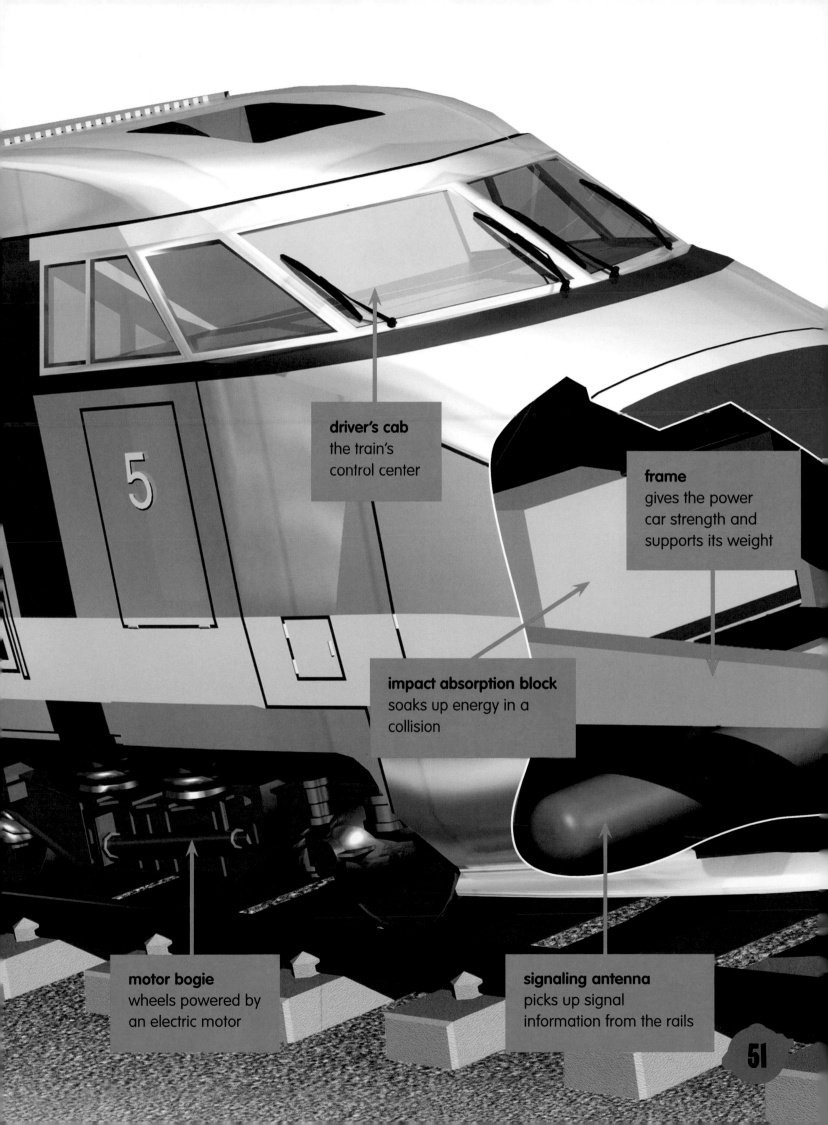

driver's cab
the train's control center

frame
gives the power car strength and supports its weight

impact absorption block
soaks up energy in a collision

motor bogie
wheels powered by an electric motor

signaling antenna
picks up signal information from the rails

TUNNEL SHUTTLES

Eurostar trains are unusual because they run under the sea! The English Channel is a body of water between the south of England and the rest of Europe. Eurostar trains travel through the Channel Tunnel, which is made up of two tunnels dug through the rock beneath the sea. These electric trains are powered by 25,000 volts of electricity from an overhead power cable. A train goes through the tunnel every four minutes, traveling between England, France, and Belgium.

FACT!
The freight locomotives that speed through the Channel Tunnel are the most powerful in the world.

Tunnel freight

A different type of train is used to carry vehicles, rather than just people, through the Channel Tunnel below the English Channel between England and France. The locomotives for these trains are more powerful than 40 family cars! Two locomotives pull a train weighing as much as 2,645 tons at speeds of up to 86 mph! Cars and vans are carried inside enclosed wagons. Trucks travel in different, open-sided wagons.

▲ Cars drive straight from the platform into rail wagons for their journey through the Channel Tunnel.

TRAFFIC CONTROL

The people who control trains in the Channel Tunnel sit in front of a giant display board. This has a map of the tunnels that shows the positions of all the trains. There is an identical control room at each end of the tunnel. If one control room has a problem, the other can take over immediately.

▲ Channel Tunnel controllers always know exactly where every single train is, and what the signals are showing.

TILTING TRAINS

When trains go around curves, passengers feel as if they are being pushed sideways. If trains go too fast, things start sliding off the tables! Because of this, trains have to slow down when they go around curves. Slowing down and speeding up again afterward wastes time and makes journeys longer. One answer is to build straighter tracks, like those used by the French TGV and the Japanese Shinkansen trains. Another answer is to build trains, such as the American Acela Express, that can tilt on curves.

Tilting trains are ➤ more comfortable for passengers at high speeds.

◄ Pendolino trains tilt automatically as the train goes around a curve in the track.

Little pendulum

Pendolino means "little **pendulum**" in Italian. It is also the name of a type of tilting train that is very popular in Europe. It is used in Portugal, Slovenia, Finland, Germany, the Czech Republic, and the United Kingdom. Several other countries plan to introduce these tilting trains in the future.

FACT!
The first tilting trains were developed in Spain in the 1930s.

57

MONORAILS

Most trains run on two steel rails, but **monorail** trains run on just one rail. This "rail" is usually a concrete **beam** that sits on towers, so the track is high above the ground. Monorail trains have two sets of wheels. One set supports the train's weight. A second set grips the beam and keeps the train upright. Most monorail trains ride on top of the rail, but there are a few that hang below the rail. The electric current for the motors comes from the rail.

FACT!

The world's first commercial monorail opened in Listowel, Ireland, in 1888.

▲ About 30,000 visitors to Las Vegas use the city's monorail to get around every day.

Hanging around

In the German city of Düsseldorf, the Sky-Train that links the airport and the railway station is a monorail. The cars hang underneath the rail, 75 feet above the ground. The rail is a hollow beam, and the train's wheels run inside it. The 1.5-mile journey takes about five minutes.

Above the busy streets of Düsseldorf, the Sky-Train ➤ whisks passengers to and from the airport.

▲ Disneyland's monorail trains carry 150,000 people every day.

DISNEY MONORAILS

Monorails have carried visitors around Walt Disney resorts since 1959. The first one opened in Disneyland in California. The trains are powered by 600 volts of electricity from the rail. Each train can sense if it is getting too close to the train in front. It warns the driver, or the train brakes automatically.

FLYERS

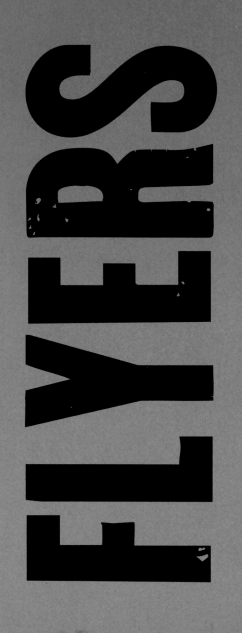

A new type of train actually flies above its track! It is called a maglev. Maglev is short for "magnetic **levitation**." The train rises up in the air by **magnetism**. There are powerful magnets in the train and also in the specially built track, or guideway. Magnetic forces between the train and the track lift the train above the track and move it along. Maglevs can go twice as fast as normal trains.

The Transrapid maglev runs on a track ➤ that is raised above the ground.

FACT!

Transrapid

The first maglev designed for passengers runs between the city of Shanghai, China, and Shanghai's international airport. It is known as the Transrapid. Passenger services began in 2004, with the train reaching a top speed of 264 mph. In tests, Transrapid maglevs have gone faster than 307 mph.

▲ Japan's sleek, futuristic MLX01 maglev is the fastest in the world.

FUTURE FLYERS

An experimental maglev in Japan has reached 361 mph on a test track with passengers on board. The MLX01 is an advanced maglev for the future. It uses special magnets called superconducting magnets. These magnets are made efficient and powerful by cooling them so that they are many times colder than ice!

61

ROLLER COASTERS

A **roller coaster** is one of the most exciting rail vehicles you can ride. Most roller coasters work by towing a line of cars up a steep hill, and then releasing them. **Gravity** pulls the cars down the other side of the hill and around the rest of the track. The latest roller coasters do not rely on gravity alone. The cars are launched along the track. This makes them go faster for an even more exciting ride!

Staying on track

Roller-coaster cars do not sit on top of their rails like railway cars. Instead, they have wheels above, below, and outside the rails, which grip the rails. The cars cannot fall off, even when they go fast around tight turns or are upside down.

▼ Roller-coaster cars pick up speed as they plunge downhill on their special track.

FACT!
Kingda Ka roller-coaster cars reach a top speed of 128 mph.

KINGDA KA

Cars on the Kingda Ka roller coaster at Six Flags Great Adventure in Jackson Township, New Jersey, are launched to the top of a 456-foot tower. Then they drop down the other side, reaching speeds of 121 mph.

Passengers on Kingda Ka become weightless ▲ for a moment as the cars plunge downward.

63

IN THE AIR

Every day, thousands of aircraft soar into the sky. There are all sorts of aircraft, and they are used for many different purposes. Some are just big enough for the pilot, and only make short flights. Others carry hundreds of people all across the world. **Airliners** carry passengers and **cargo** planes transport goods and materials between the world's biggest airports. Search-and-rescue helicopters help people in trouble, and **experimental** planes test new ideas.

▲ A paramotor pilot steers by pulling control lines to change the shape of the parachute.

KEEP IT SIMPLE

The simplest aircraft with an engine is a paramotor. Its engine is very small and drives a propeller that has a metal frame around it. The pilot straps the engine to his back and hangs under a wing-shaped parachute, called a paraglider. The pilot uses a hand controller to make the engine go faster or slower.

Building planes

Airliners are complicated machines. Each one is built from thousands of parts. First, large pieces of each plane are built separately, and then cranes bring these pieces to one place so that they can be joined together. After this, the electrical and **control systems** are added, and the engines are fitted. Finally, the seats are put in and the plane is painted.

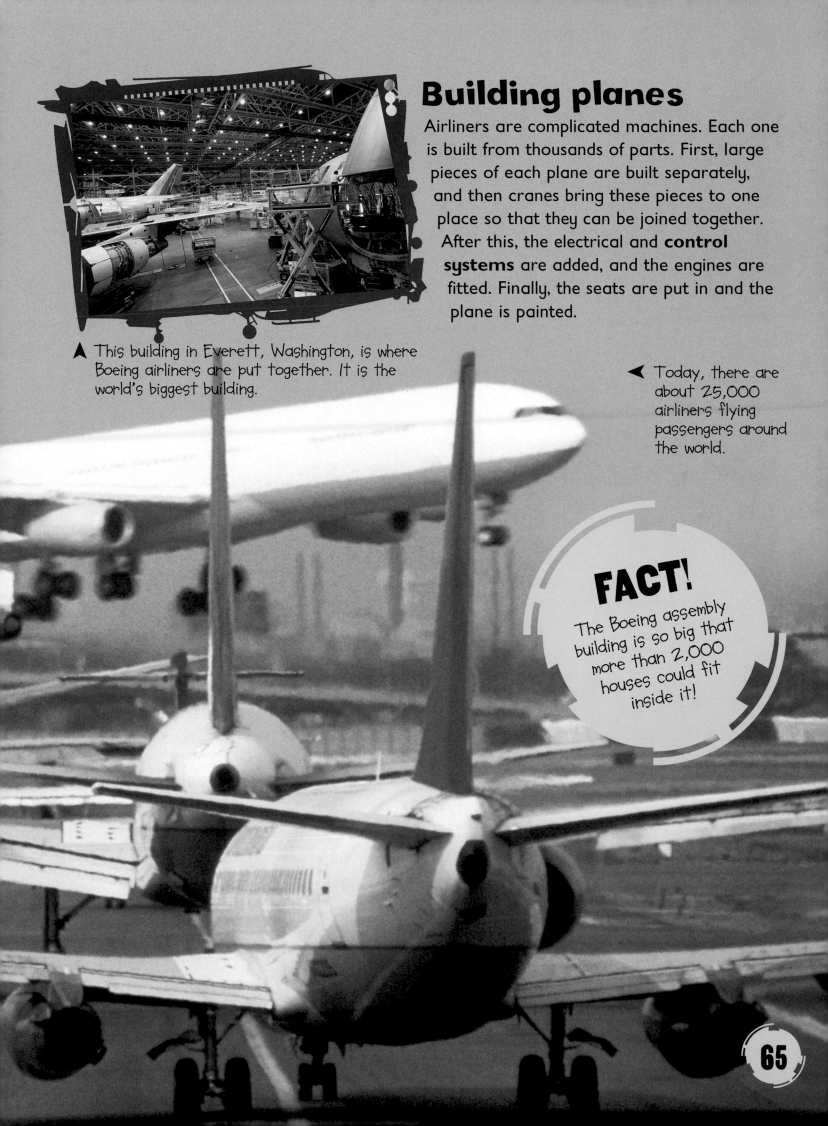

▲ This building in Everett, Washington, is where Boeing airliners are put together. It is the world's biggest building.

◀ Today, there are about 25,000 airliners flying passengers around the world.

FACT!

The Boeing assembly building is so big that more than 2,000 houses could fit inside it!

FUN PLANES

Flying a plane is great fun. Lots of planes are flown simply because their pilots enjoy flying so much. Many pilots fly very small planes. These planes have engines that work like car engines, but they drive a propeller instead of wheels. Some pilots like to fly planes called **gliders**. They do not have any engines at all, and they glide through the sky like a bird!

Pilots learn to fly in small ➤ aircraft like this.

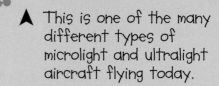
▲ This is one of the many different types of microlight and ultralight aircraft flying today.

MICRO FLYING

The smallest planes are called microlights, **ultralights,** or **light sport aircraft. It is easier for people to afford one of these planes of their own. The simplest microlights have an open frame, with a seat and an engine. Others have a covering over the body and** cockpit.

Sailing on air

How do gliders fly if they do not have engines? A glider is often towed into the air by a cable attached to another plane. The cable is released when the glider is flying. The pilot then looks for **air currents** to carry the glider higher and to keep it flying for longer. To land, the pilot gradually comes back to the ground.

A glider's long, thin wings are a great shape for soaring. ▲

BIZ-JETS

Business people sometimes choose to travel in small planes called **business jets**, or biz-jets, so they can fly at a time that suits them best. Most biz-jets carry four to ten passengers. They can fly into small airports where bigger airliners cannot land. Even though they are small, biz-jets can still cost millions of dollars. Some businesses cut the cost by sharing biz-jets, or by hiring them only when they need them.

Gulfstream

The Gulfstream 100 is a business jet with room for two pilots and up to seven passengers. Its power comes from twin **jet engines** at its rear. It can fly from New York to most airports in North America. From Rome, Italy, it can reach airports in Europe, Scandinavia, and North Africa.

◄ The Gulfstream 100 is the smallest of the Gulfsteam business jets.

FLYING OFFICES

It is hard for passengers to do any work in a crowded airliner. But business jets can be used as flying offices. Meetings can be held and office work done during a flight. The passenger cabin may be small, but there is enough room for comfortable seats and tables to work on.

▲ A biz-jet cabin is small compared to that of an airliner, but it is comfortable and convenient.

▲ The CitationJet is a light business jet for journeys up to 1,700 miles.

FACT!
There are more than 20,000 business jets flying in the world today.

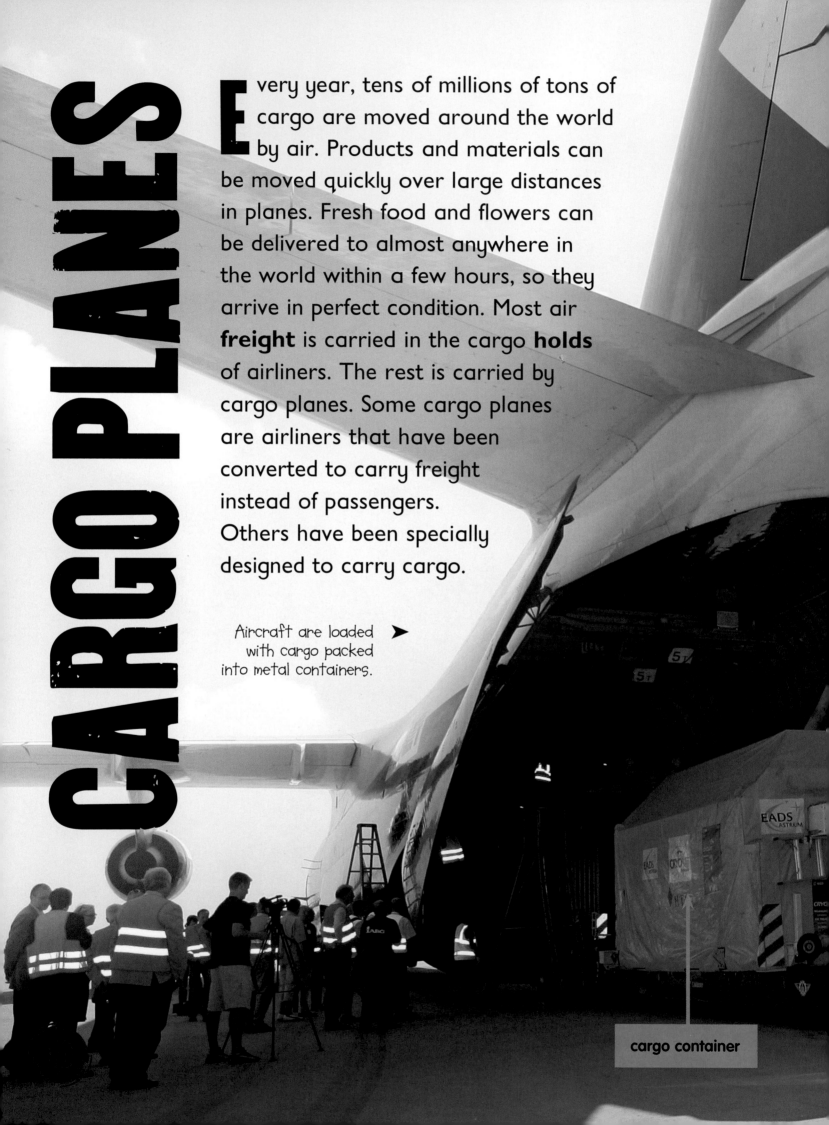

CARGO PLANES

Every year, tens of millions of tons of cargo are moved around the world by air. Products and materials can be moved quickly over large distances in planes. Fresh food and flowers can be delivered to almost anywhere in the world within a few hours, so they arrive in perfect condition. Most air **freight** is carried in the cargo **holds** of airliners. The rest is carried by cargo planes. Some cargo planes are airliners that have been converted to carry freight instead of passengers. Others have been specially designed to carry cargo.

Aircraft are loaded ➤ with cargo packed into metal containers.

cargo container

Super transporter

The Airbus A300-600ST Super Transporter has the biggest cargo hold of any aircraft. It is such an enormous plane that it is also called the Beluga, after a large type of whale. The Airbus Super Transporter is a specially modified Airbus airliner. It carries parts of other Airbus aircraft to the factory where the planes are put together.

▲ Airbus has five of these huge transport planes.

FACT!

The world's biggest **mass-produced** cargo plane is the Antonov An-124 Ruslan. It is built in Ukraine, a country in eastern Europe.

WARPLANES

Planes play an important role in war. Different types of warplanes do different jobs. Fighters attack other planes, bombers attack targets on the ground, and fighter-bombers can do both of these jobs. Special spy planes are used to find out information that might help to win a war. The latest warplanes are made from materials that do not show up well on **radar**, which is used to spot enemy planes. These planes are called stealth planes. The F-22 fighter and B-2 bomber are stealth planes.

Modern fighter

The F-22 Raptor is the world's newest fighter plane. The U.S. Air Force first used it in 2005. It can fly at twice the **speed of sound** up to seven miles above the ground, and is designed to outperform any other fighter it might meet in the air.

The big opening ▶ on each side of the F-22 takes in lots of air for the plane's engines.

air intake

cockpit

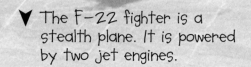
▼ The F-22 fighter is a stealth plane. It is powered by two jet engines.

▲ The Global Hawk spy plane does not have a cockpit because it does not need a pilot!

ROBOT PLANE

The Global Hawk is a spy plane without a pilot! Its computers are programmed with a mission before it takes off. The Global Hawk carries out the mission and then returns to the base all by itself. It can circle over one spot for up to 24 hours—for longer than any plane flown by a human pilot.

FACT!

In 2001, a Global Hawk spy plane flew itself 8,600 miles, from the United States to Australia.

HOVER FLIES

Most aircraft have to move along the ground very fast before their wings can lift them up into the sky. These aircraft need a long, straight runway to help them get into the air. But there are some aircraft that can fly straight up and even **hover** in one place. Some of these aircraft are planes, but most of them are helicopters. A helicopter's **rotor blades** whirl around like long, thin wings to lift the aircraft straight up into the air.

FACT!

The Harrier Jump Jet was the first successful military **vertical** takeoff plane.

Heli-plane

The Bell BA609 Tiltrotor has enormous propellers. This is because they are not just propellers. When the aircraft is on the ground, the spinning propellers lift it straight upward, like a helicopter. Then the engines tilt forward and the Tiltrotor flies like a normal plane. The BA609 doesn't need a runway to take off and land.

tilting engine

▲ The Bell BA609 Tiltrotor begins to tilt its propellers to the front so that it can fly forward.

◄ A helicopter can land almost anywhere. It can land on a road or a field, or even on an oil rig at sea.

FUTURE FIGHTER

The F-35 fighter is an exciting plane for the future. Three different versions of the F-35 will be built: one for the U.S. Air Force, one for the U.S. Navy, and another for the U.S. Marines. The Marines' plane will be able to take off and land vertically, like a helicopter.

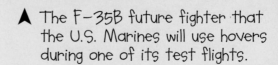

▲ The F-35B future fighter that the U.S. Marines will use hovers during one of its test flights.

75

wings
measure 262 feet from tip to tip

fuselage
where the passengers sit—it's 23 feet wide

AIRBUS A38

windows

doors

▲ A fully loaded Airbus A380 can weigh up to 617 tons.

FACT!

Airbus A380

In 2005, an airliner even bigger than the Jumbo Jet made its first flight. The Airbus A380 is a giant plane that carries more than 550 passengers on two decks, one above the other. It is so big that there is enough space left over for an office, a gym, and even stores! It can fly up to 9,320 miles before it has to land for **fuel**. When a new airliner is designed, it has to have many tests on the ground and in the air before it is allowed to carry passengers. Five A380 airliners made test flights totaling about 2,500 hours.

cockpit
where the pilots sit and control the aircraft

▲ The double-decker Airbus A380 is the biggest airliner ever built.

First flight

The Airbus A380's **maiden flight** on April 27, 2005, was a success. It lasted nearly four hours. The plane carried a crew of six and about 22 tons of test equipment. Experts on the ground watched live pictures sent from the plane's **flight deck**.

More than 50,000 people ➤ gathered at Toulouse, France, to see the A380's first flight.

AIRLINERS

Every year, nearly 2 billion people fly in an airliner. The biggest airliners fly people on the busiest routes between the world's largest international airports. Smaller planes fly between both international airports and smaller airports in different areas or cities. For about 30 years, the world's biggest airliner has been the Boeing 747. It is so big that it was quickly nicknamed the "**Jumbo Jet**." The biggest type of Jumbo Jet is the Boeing 747-400.

Boeing 777

The latest Boeing airliner is the 777. It was the first airliner designed totally on computers, without any drawings made on paper. When the first Boeing 747 was produced in the 1960s, it needed 75,000 paper drawings! The designers of the new 777 could move its parts around on computer screens to check that they would fit together before the plane was built.

▲ The Boeing 777 has two of the biggest and most powerful jet engines ever fitted to an airliner.

GLASS COCKPITS

In the 1970s, airliner cockpits were crammed with hundreds of instruments and controls, but today you will mainly see computer screens instead. A cockpit with computer screens is also known as a glass cockpit.

Modern airliners have glass cockpits with up to six computer screens. ➤

computer screen

Each wing of a Boeing 747-400 ▲ airliner is big enough for 45 cars to park on.

FACT!
The Boeing 747's enormous passenger cabin is so big that the first-ever plane flight in 1903 could have been made inside it!

BUILDING THE A380

A380 parts are carried by barge, ship, plane, and truck to the assembly plant in Toulouse, France. The world's biggest airliner is built in an enormous building 1,680 feet long, 820 feet wide, and 150 feet high. It has eight huge sliding doors, big enough for planes to fit through.

The building where A380 airliners are put together covers as much area as 25 football fields. ➤

Safety tests

Lots of safety features are built into the A380. They all have to be tested to make sure that they work properly. All the passengers have to be able to escape from the plane within only 90 seconds, with just half the doors open. The A380 passed this test.

In an emergency on the ground, passengers use slides to leave the plane quickly. ➤

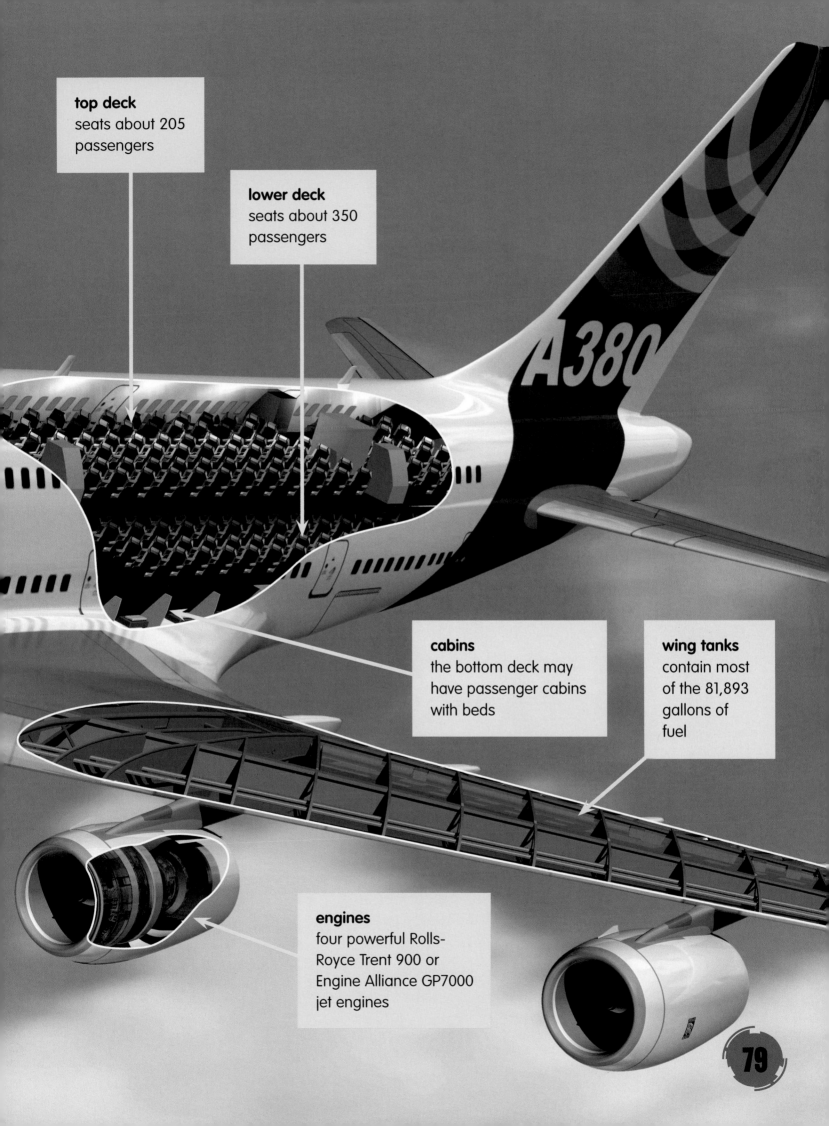

top deck
seats about 205 passengers

lower deck
seats about 350 passengers

cabins
the bottom deck may have passenger cabins with beds

wing tanks
contain most of the 81,893 gallons of fuel

engines
four powerful Rolls-Royce Trent 900 or Engine Alliance GP7000 jet engines

COMPETITION PLANES

In the days when there were very few planes, people flocked to air shows and air races to see pilots competing against each other. The winning pilots were as famous as pop stars are now! Air races are still held today. The planes race around an imaginary track in the sky. The track is marked out by towers, called pylons, on the ground. There are **aerobatic** competitions, too. Aerobatic pilots make amazing tumbling, looping **stunts** in the air.

FACT!

The Pitts Special stunt plane made its first flight in 1944.

Stunt flying

The Pitts Special stunt plane has won more aerobatic competitions than any other aircraft. It is a biplane, which means that it has two sets of wings, one above the other. It is a very strong plane that can turn and spin in the sky without breaking apart.

◄ There are more modern aerobatic planes, but the Pitts Special can still put on a great show.

EXTRA FUN

The Extra 300 is a modern high-performance aerobatic plane. The pilot can roll it all the way around, from right way up to upside down and back again, in less than one second! It can perform very exciting stunts.

▲ Its small size, light weight, and powerful engine make the Extra 300 very **nimble**.

▲ Competition planes make a tight turn in an air race.

LIGHTER THAN AIR

The first aircraft that people flew in were hot-air balloons and **airships**, which are known as lighter-than-air (LTA) craft. LTA craft rise up into the sky because they are filled with gases that make them lighter than air. Airships are filled with a very light gas called helium. Hot-air balloons are filled with air that is hotter than the air around them. The pilot heats the air inside the balloon with a gas flame.

Airships today

The Zeppelin NT is a modern airship made in Germany. Up to 14 people, including two crew members, sit in a cabin called a **gondola**, underneath the airship. The weight of the airship is balanced by the lighter-than-air helium gas inside it. The airship is made to take off or come down again by tilting its propellers up or down.

▲ The Zeppelin NT airship made its first flight in 1997.

84

HOT AIR

Hot-air balloons drift silently with the wind. The pilot and passengers stand in a basket under the balloon. The pilot makes the balloon climb by turning on a gas flame to heat the air inside the balloon. Turning the flame off lets the air cool, so the balloon goes down again.

Most balloons are round, but they ► can be made in all sorts of shapes.

gondola

FACT!

In the 1930s, people traveled between Europe and the United States in huge luxury airships.

▲ Airships are used to keep an eye on traffic and to film important events on the ground below.

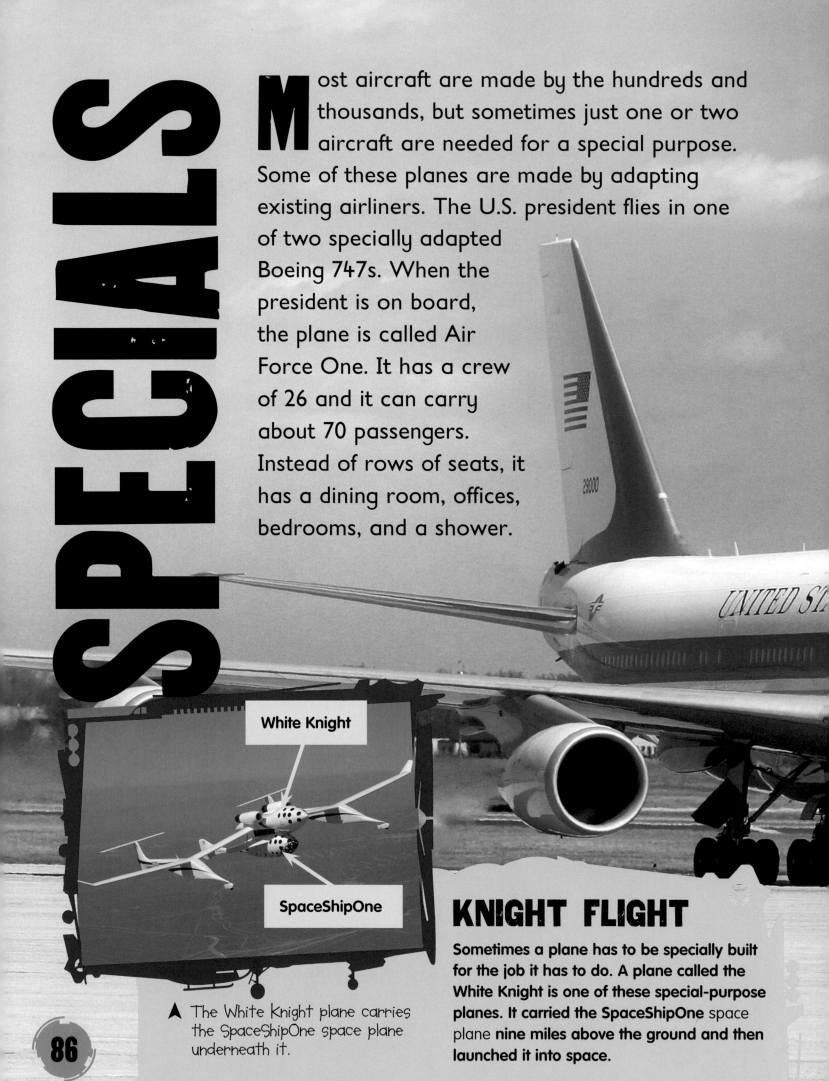

SPECIALS

Most aircraft are made by the hundreds and thousands, but sometimes just one or two aircraft are needed for a special purpose. Some of these planes are made by adapting existing airliners. The U.S. president flies in one of two specially adapted Boeing 747s. When the president is on board, the plane is called Air Force One. It has a crew of 26 and it can carry about 70 passengers. Instead of rows of seats, it has a dining room, offices, bedrooms, and a shower.

White Knight

SpaceShipOne

▲ The White Knight plane carries the SpaceShipOne space plane underneath it.

KNIGHT FLIGHT

Sometimes a plane has to be specially built for the job it has to do. A plane called the White Knight is one of these special-purpose planes. It carried the SpaceShipOne space plane nine miles above the ground and then launched it into space.

Vomit Comet

"Vomit Comet" is the nickname of a plane used by **NASA** to let trainee astronauts feel what it is like to be weightless. As the plane dives toward the ground, the passengers float about inside its padded passenger cabin. The European and Russian space agencies have Vomit Comets, too.

◀ Vomit Comet passengers can fly about as if they weigh nothing. It makes some passengers feel sick!

▲ Air Force One is the U.S. president's official plane.

FACT!

The biggest plane ever built is the Antonov An-225. It is so big that it could carry the Russian space shuttle on its back!

LONG-DISTANCE

Aircraft have been setting records for as long as they have existed. There were always pilots who wanted to go faster, higher, and farther than anyone else. The longest distance records are set by planes that have to be specially built to keep flying for several days without landing. They have to be as light as possible, but also very strong, because they need to carry an enormous amount of fuel for the long journey.

The GlobalFlyer long-distance aircraft is powered by one small jet engine above the cockpit. ➤

fuel tanks

FACT!
At takeoff, the GlobalFlyer carried more than four times its own weight in fuel!

Going solo

In 2005, Steve Fossett became the first person to fly around the world nonstop on his own. He flew a specially designed aircraft called the GlobalFlyer. In 2006, Fossett broke another record when he made the longest-ever flight without stopping, again in the GlobalFlyer. He flew a distance of 26,388 miles in just over 76 hours.

▲ In 2005, Steve Fossett completed the first nonstop around-the-world flight in 67 hours.

jet engine

cockpit

Superliner

Airliners sometimes set records, too. In 2004, an Airbus A340-500 made the longest flight by any airliner. It flew 10,315 miles from Singapore to New York. It can make such long flights because it has bigger wings and a smaller, lighter body than other liners. It carries so much fuel that the fuel weighs ten times as much as the passengers!

▲ The long-distance Airbus A340-500 could fly nonstop all the way from London, England, to Perth, Australia!

89

EXPERIMENTAL

When scientists and engineers want to test a new type of engine or a new shape for a plane, they sometimes build an experimental plane especially for the tests. A famous series of experimental planes is called the **X-planes**. They have been built in the United States since the 1940s to test all sorts of new aircraft. The first one, X-1, was the first plane to fly faster than the speed of sound. Others have tested new vertical takeoff planes, jet planes, **rocket**-powered planes, and space planes.

Superspeeder

Today, airliners fly just below the speed of sound. In the future, some airliners might fly as fast as ten times the speed of sound, or about 6,835 mph. NASA is using a flying model called X-43A to test a new type of engine, called a **scramjet**, for these fast planes.

A future airliner ➤ flying at ten times the speed of sound might look like this.

LOOK, NO BODY!

Future airliners might not have a tail or a body! Instead, passengers would sit inside its wings. This type of plane is called a Blended Wing Body (BWB). So far, only models of the X-48 Blended Wing Body have been made for tests.

A model of a future ▶ airliner is being tested.

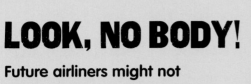
solar panels

▼ NASA's Helios experimental **solar-powered** aircraft makes a test flight.

AeroVironment In
HELIOS

NASA ERAST
AeroVironment Inc.
HELIOS

NASA ERAST
AeroVironment Inc.
HELIOS

FACT!

At ten times the speed of sound, you could fly from London, England, to Sydney, Australia, in only two hours!

MACHINES IN WATER

People have traveled on water using boats and ships for thousands of years. Today, **ferries** and **liners** carry passengers all over the world, cargo ships move goods and materials across the oceans, warships fight at sea, **powerboats** compete in exciting races, and many people spend their free time on small sailboats and **cruise ships**. These water machines range in size from small boats the size of a car to huge ships the size of a skyscraper lying on its side!

THE PARTS OF A SHIP

The hull is the part of a ship that sits in the water. Narrow-shaped hulls can slice through water quickly, but wider hulls hold more passengers and cargo. The sharp front end of the hull is called the bow and the back end is the stern. The ship's control center is called the bridge. This is raised high above the rest of the ship so the captain can get a good view.

All ships, like this cruise ➤ liner, have a bow, a stern, a hull, and a bridge.

bridge

stern

bow

hull

Water power

Most boats and ships have **propellers** to push them through the water. The propeller of a small boat is so tiny that it can be held in the palm of your hand. The propeller of a huge liner or cargo ship can be as big as a house!

▲ Powerful engines drive the huge propellers of a large ship.

◄ Big ships are made by covering a metal frame with sheets of metal.

OCEAN LINERS

In the days before air travel became popular, travelers crossed the oceans in ships called liners. The great liners had names like *France*, *Normandie*, *United States*, and *Queen Elizabeth*. They competed with each other to cross the oceans in the shortest time. The fastest ones could make the crossing in four or five days.

FACT!

The RMS **Titanic** was built in 1912. It was the biggest and fastest transatlantic liner of its time. Tragically, it hit an iceberg and sank on its first voyage.

The **Queen Mary II** ➤ set sail for the first time in 2004. With over 1,000 cabins, this is the biggest passenger liner built to date.

SUPER LINER

At 1,132 feet long—the length of more than 40 buses—the *Queen Mary II* can carry over 2,500 passengers. The liner is powered by four giant diesel engines and two gas engines similar to aircraft jet engines. Between them, they make enough electricity to light a city!

◄ If you could stand the **Queen Mary II** on one end, it would be almost as tall as the Empire State Building in New York City.

Floating resorts

Modern liners are like floating luxury hotels. They have stores, swimming pools, restaurants, and even movie theaters to keep passengers entertained during the voyage.

◄ Modern passenger liners are incredibly luxurious— they are like grand hotels on water!

FERRIES

Ferries are passenger ships that carry people to and from ports on short sea routes. Some ferries carry vehicles as well as passengers. These ships have large doors in either the bow or stern. When the ship docks, the doors open wide and the vehicles inside it drive out. This type of ferry is called a **roll-on, roll-off ferry,** or "ro-ro" for short.

Car ferries can carry ➤ many cars and their passengers. They are like huge floating parking garages!

▼ The **Ulysses** weighs more than 50,000 tons. This giant ferry has 12 decks and is so tall that it towers over other ships.

SUPER FERRIES

Some ferries are huge. *Ulysses* belongs to the Irish Ferries fleet and can carry more vehicles than any other ferry in the world. Inside, there are almost three miles of parking spaces—that's enough room for over 1,300 cars. *Ulysses* can also carry 2,000 passengers.

High-speed ferries

Most ferries move slowly, but some are designed to be extremely fast. Many of the fast ferries have two hulls instead of one and are called **catamarans**.

With their twin ➤ hulls, catamarans travel twice as fast as other ferries.

FACT!
A ferry called Cat-Link V made the fastest-ever crossing of the Atlantic Ocean in July 1998. Its voyage took 2 days, 20 hours, and 9 minutes.

FISHING BOATS

Fishing boats are powerful **vessels** with a broad, deep hull that can hold many fish. Small boats work close to the coast, and bigger vessels fish farther away in the deep ocean. Some fishing boats can freeze their catch on board.

FINDING FISH

The ocean is a big place, so how do fishermen know where to find fish? They use special equipment that helps them locate large shoals, or groups, of fish. Sonar **sends sound waves down into the water and helps the fishermen "see" underwater.**

▲ Fish shoals found by sonar equipment are shown on a screen on board the fishing boat.

Fishing gear

Fishing boats drag their nets behind them. The shapes and sizes of the nets used, and their depth in the water, depend on the type of fish the fishermen want to catch. Some fish are found near the seabed, but others swim in shoals closer to the surface. The fish are trapped in nets, and the nets are then pulled onto the ship.

▲ Fishing boats use powerful **hoists** and **winches** to pull the catch onto the deck.

Fishing boats need ➤ engines with lots of pulling power to tow the heavy nets through the water.

SAILING BOATS

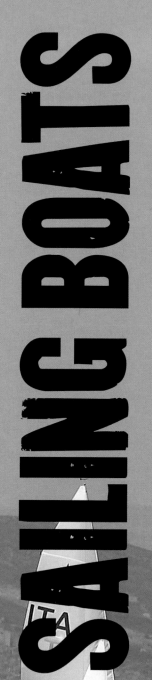

Sailboats use wind power to move themselves forward. The most advanced yachts compete in international races and set new speed records. Designed by computers, these boats may have one, two, or even three hulls. Their hulls and **masts** are made from modern materials like **carbon fiber** to make them strong and light.

The yachts taking part in this race are all the same, so the race will be won by the most skilled crew. ➤

FACT!
The speed record for a sailboat is 53.5 mph. It was set in 1993 by a yacht called **Yellow Pages Endeavour.**

Racing catamarans

Many racing yachts are twin-hulled boats called catamarans. Two thin hulls slice through water faster than one big hull. They also give the boat a wider base and make it harder for the wind to blow it over.

▲ Sailors push racing catamarans to their limit when trying to go as fast as possible in competitions.

SPEED RECORDS

Britain's Ellen MacArthur set a series of speed records in 2004 and 2005 in her specially built trimaran. It had a long, slender central hull to help it slice through the water at high speeds.

Ellen MacArthur's ➤ record–breaking trimaran is a special water machine. It has a float on each side to keep the wind and waves from rolling it over.

POWERBOATS

Powerboats come in all shapes and sizes, from small motor cruisers and sporty speedboats to incredibly fast racing machines. Many powerboats have a sharp, V-shaped hull that slices through the water. Others have a flat-bottomed hull that skims the water's surface, allowing the boat to travel even faster. These surface skimmers are called **hydroplanes**. Personal water vehicles, better known as Jet Skis, also dart along the surface at top speeds, almost like floating motorcycles!

Offshore powerboat racers ▶ have incredibly powerful engines that can be up to five times more powerful than that of an ordinary car.

JUST ADD WATER

GUERNSEY

FACT!

The highest speed ever reached on water is 317.6 mph. It was set in 1978 by Ken Warby in his hydroplane Spirit of Australia.

Ski boats

Some speedboats, called ski boats, are specially designed for towing water-skiers and **wakeboarder**s through the water at breathtaking speeds. A wide, flat hull allows ski boats to move at fast speeds across the surface of the water.

▲ Ski boats glide over the water's surface at fast speeds. This is called "planing."

◄ A Jet Ski rider steers by turning the handlebars and leaning to one side.

SKIMMING RACERS

As a hydroplane racing boat picks up speed, it rises up on top of the water—planing like a ski boat. At top speed, only the propeller and the tips of two floats are in the water.

The fastest racing hydroplanes can reach speeds of about 200 mph. ►

satellite system
uses space satellites to track the ship's exact position

bridge
the ship's control center

helm
the place where the **helmsman** stands to steer the ship

large windows
give the bridge officers a clear view

crane
lifts heavy pipes that load and unload the cargo

lifeboat

rudder
turns to steer the ship

diesel engine
burns diesel oil to turn the ship's propeller

hull
a 6½-foot-thick double hull—one hull sits inside another

GAS TANKERS

Gas tankers are ships that are designed to carry gas. Before it is loaded onto a tanker, the gas is first cooled to change it into a liquid. Liquid takes up less space, which means the tanker can carry more. Liquid natural gas and liquid petroleum are transported like this.

The tanks of a ➤ gas carrier ship are surrounded by thick **insulation**, which keeps the cargo cold.

smokestack releases fumes and smoke from the engines

NO SMOKING

Building a cargo ship

The first part of a cargo ship to be built is the keel. The keel is the strongest part of the ship. It runs along the bottom of the hull from the bow to the stern. A frame of steel beams is built upward from the keel and covered with steel plates to form the hull. Next, the **decks** are added. Finally a crane lifts the bridge and crew cabins into position.

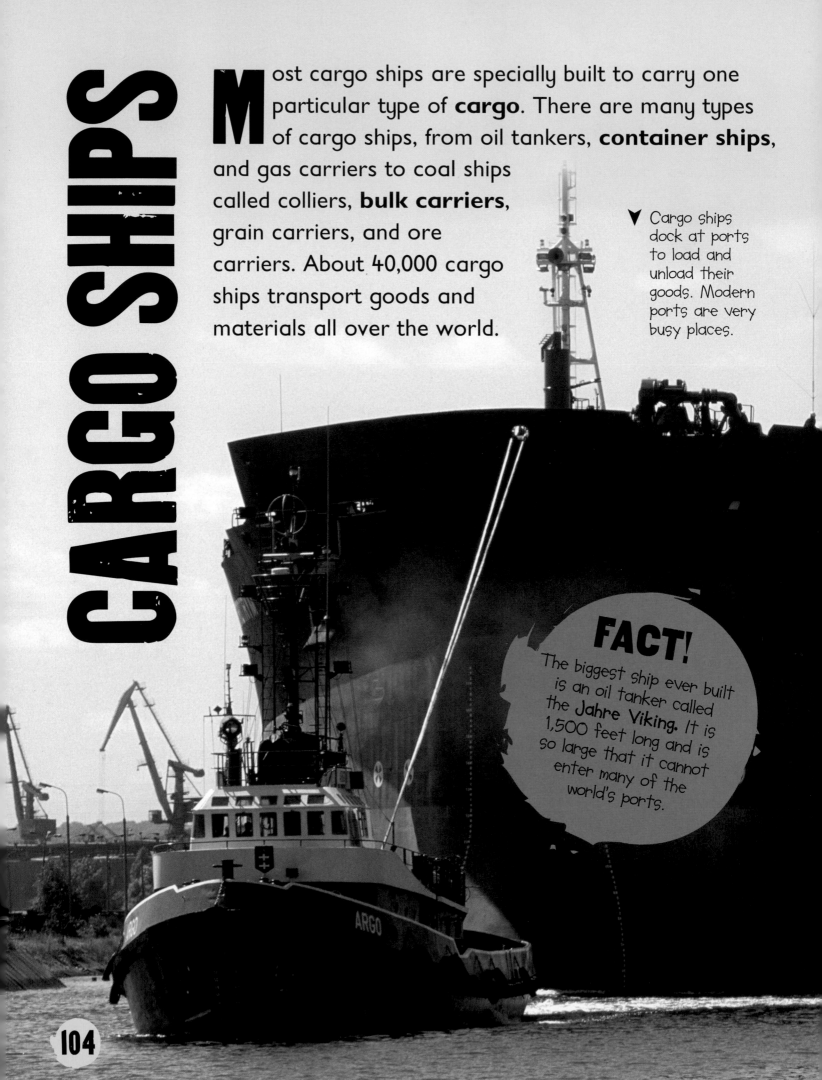

CARGO SHIPS

Most cargo ships are specially built to carry one particular type of **cargo**. There are many types of cargo ships, from oil tankers, **container ships**, and gas carriers to coal ships called colliers, **bulk carriers**, grain carriers, and ore carriers. About 40,000 cargo ships transport goods and materials all over the world.

▼ Cargo ships dock at ports to load and unload their goods. Modern ports are very busy places.

FACT!

The biggest ship ever built is an oil tanker called the Jahre Viking. It is 1,500 feet long and is so large that it cannot enter many of the world's ports.

Tugboats

There is little spare space in a busy port. This can make it difficult for big ships to move around. Some cargo ships have extra propellers called **thrusters** to help them turn in a tight space and sometimes dock by themselves. Ships can also be moved around safely by small but powerful boats called **tugboats**.

▲ **Tides** and wind can make a big cargo ship difficult to control. Tugboats often move them in and out of ports.

▼ The job of a port traffic controller is to make sure that ships enter and leave port safely.

TRAFFIC CONTROL

Like many modern ships, cargo ships use satellites to navigate, or find their way around. Radio signals from satellites orbiting the earth show exactly where ships are located and where they are heading. When cargo ships enter busy shipping lanes near big ports, their movements are strictly controlled to avoid collisions.

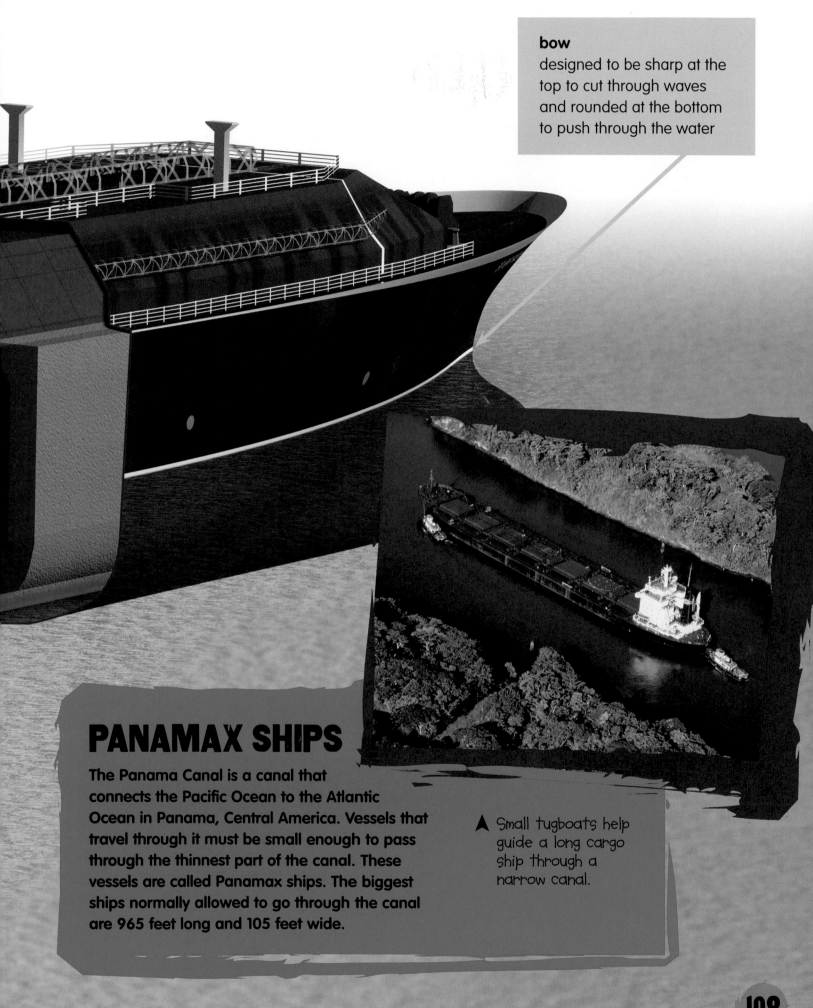

bow
designed to be sharp at the top to cut through waves and rounded at the bottom to push through the water

PANAMAX SHIPS

The Panama Canal is a canal that connects the Pacific Ocean to the Atlantic Ocean in Panama, Central America. Vessels that travel through it must be small enough to pass through the thinnest part of the canal. These vessels are called Panamax ships. The biggest ships normally allowed to go through the canal are 965 feet long and 105 feet wide.

▲ Small tugboats help guide a long cargo ship through a narrow canal.

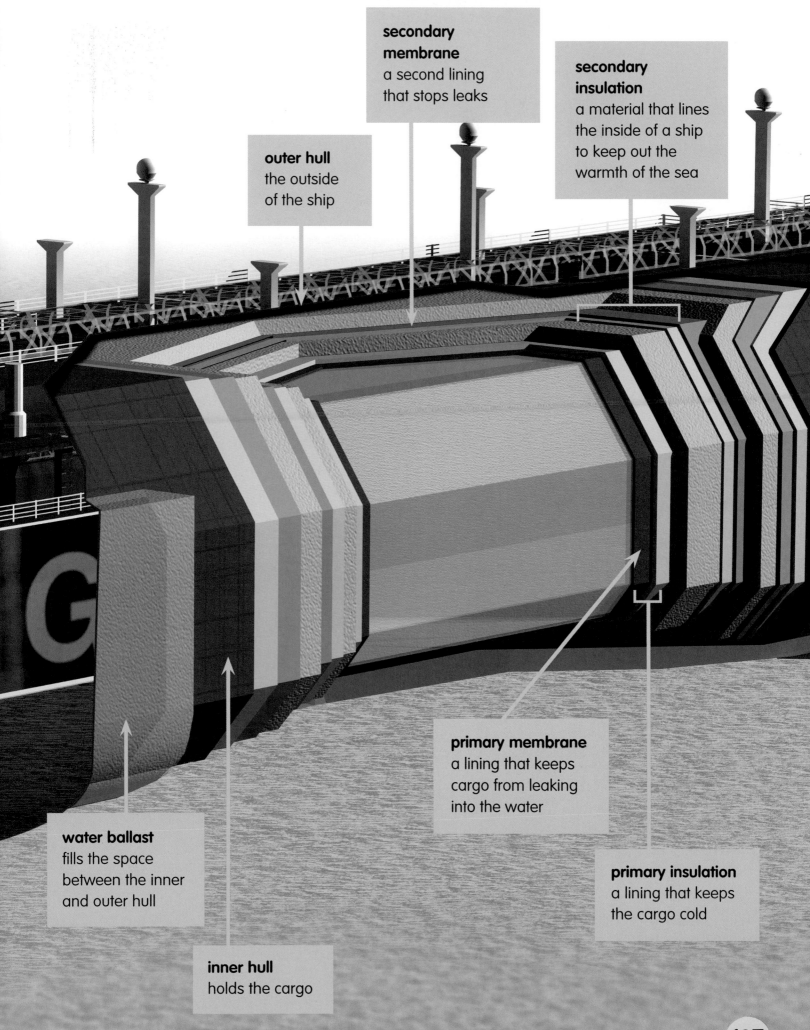

secondary membrane
a second lining
that stops leaks

outer hull
the outside
of the ship

secondary insulation
a material that lines
the inside of a ship
to keep out the
warmth of the sea

primary membrane
a lining that keeps
cargo from leaking
into the water

primary insulation
a lining that keeps
the cargo cold

water ballast
fills the space
between the inner
and outer hull

inner hull
holds the cargo

FLYING BOATS

When a boat moves forward, water presses against it and slows it down. To travel faster, the hull needs to be out of the water. That's how **hydrofoil**s and **hovercraft** travel. Hydrofoils have underwater wings called **foils**. As they speed up, the hull starts to rise and comes out of the water altogether.

With their ➤ underwater wings, hydrofoils provide fast passenger transportation on rivers and lakes, and between islands.

▼ A Boeing Jetfoil cruises over the water at up to 50 mph.

Jetfoils

Jetfoils are hydrofoils powered by **waterjet** engines instead of propellers. They pump water out of the boat's stern at a high speed. The boat constantly measures its height above the water and adjusts the angle of the foils to keep it flying along at the same height.

HOVERCRAFT

Hovercraft fly over the surface of the water and can cross land and ice just as easily. They are used for search-and-rescue work, scientific research, carrying passengers, and racing.

▲ Unlike boats, passenger hovercraft do not need to tie up at the dockside— they just glide up onto the shore.

FACT!

The hovercraft was invented in the 1950s by Sir Christopher Cockerell of England. The first hovercraft, SRNI, was built in 1959.

Racing hovercraft ▶ are powered by a big propeller that spins behind the driver. A small, one-person racing craft can reach speeds of more than 65 mph.

WARSHIPS

Warships were once large, heavily armored vessels with lots of big guns. Their guns could fire shells over great distances, making them fearsome fighting machines. Today, **missiles** have replaced big guns, and the thick, heavy armor is gone, too. Most modern warships are smaller, lighter ships called **cruisers**, **destroyers**, and **frigates**. Some warships carry helicopters to search for enemy submarines.

FACT!

A modern cruiser costs over $1 billion to build!

▲ Modern warships work on their own or together with other ships in a force called a battle group.

◄ Most modern warships travel at speeds of up to 40 mph.

SUPPLY SHIPS

Warships do not always have time to visit a port to take fuel, food, and other supplies on board. Instead, supplies are delivered to them at sea by other ships. Supply ships include fuel tankers, stores ships, ammunition ships, and support ships.

▲ A warship (right) is refueled at sea by a fuel tanker (left).

113

AIRCRAFT CARRIERS

The biggest warships ever built are the U.S. Navy's Nimitz-class aircraft carriers. These **nuclear-powered warships** weigh an amazing 90,000 tons and carry a crew of about 6,000. They can hold around 85 aircraft, many of which are kept in a vast **hangar** belowdecks. When planes are needed, they are moved up to the flight deck by four huge elevators.

▼ A Nimitz–class aircraft carrier can sail for up to five years before its nuclear engines need to be refueled.

FACT!

The cooks on board a Nimitz–class aircraft carrier have to prepare up to 20,000 meals every day!

The island

An aircraft carrier is controlled from a structure on one side of the deck called the island. This keeps the deck clear for planes to land.

The island gives the ship's commander a good view of the deck and all around the ship. ▶

Landing by wire

Planes land so fast on the ship that they cannot stop before they run out of deck. Special wires, called **arrester cables**, stretch across the deck. As the plane lands, a hook under its tail catches the cables, preventing the plane from going forward.

▲ An aircraft carrier's arrester cables can stop a plane landing at 150 mph in less than 350 feet.

115

SUBMARINES

Submarines are the only naval vessels that deliberately sink themselves! They patrol the oceans, hidden beneath the waves. Submarines **submerge** soon after they leave port and stay underwater for up to three months. They only need to come to the surface when the crew runs out of food. Submarines have to be manned 24 hours a day, so there are always at least two crews on board. As one crew sleeps, the other runs the submarine.

The biggest ➤ submarines have crews of more than 150 people.

BELOW THE WAVES

Submarines have to make themselves heavier to submerge. They do this by letting seawater flood into empty tanks inside them. The biggest submarines have to take in thousands of tons of water to submerge. How do they float up to the surface again? By blowing out the water!

▲ A submarine's smooth black hull glides through the water.

Sound safety

Submarines do not have windows, so the crew uses a system called sonar to find their way around. By using sonar, the crew can probe the water ahead for objects such as underwater mountains. They can also hear the sounds of nearby ships and other submarines—and even the singing of whales!

▲ A submarine crew uses state-of-the-art technology to figure out their depth, speed, and direction.

▼ The wings on this Australian Collins-class submarine are hydroplanes. They tilt to make the sub go up or down underwater.

FACT!
The biggest submarines are Russian Typhoon-class vessels. They are 561 feet long and weigh more than 20,400 tons!

SUBMERSIBLES

Scientists and underwater explorers sometimes dive in small craft called **submersibles**. A submersible is carried by a larger ship to the place where it is to dive. When it sinks below the waves, small propellers, or thrusters, move it around. Deep-diving submersibles have just enough room inside for two or three people. They sit inside a compartment shaped like a ball, which resists the crushing pressure of the water.

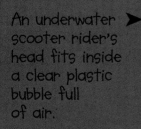

An underwater ➤ scooter rider's head fits inside a clear plastic bubble full of air.

Seeing the sights

Vacationers in some parts of the world can visit the seabed in a submersible. They can see the underwater sights, tour a tropical reef, or watch divers feeding fish.

◀ Alvin is a submersible that can dive to a depth of 2.8 miles. It was used to explore the wreck of the Titanic on the ocean floor.

FLYING UNDERWATER

A little like balloons, most submersibles sink and surface by making themselves heavier or lighter. But a new type of submersible actually "flies" underwater in the same way that a plane flies through the air—it even has wings!

◀ Deep Flight 1 is a new kind of submersible with wings. It was developed to explore the deepest parts of the ocean.

IN SPACE

The Space Age began on October 4, 1957, when the first **satellite**, *Sputnik I*, was sent into space. A satellite is a kind of spacecraft that travels around Earth or other planets. Some spacecraft are manned—they have people inside. Others, such as satellites, are unmanned. Some satellites take photographs of Earth. Others send television pictures and telephone messages to different parts of the world. Scientists use satellites to study our planet and the rest of the universe.

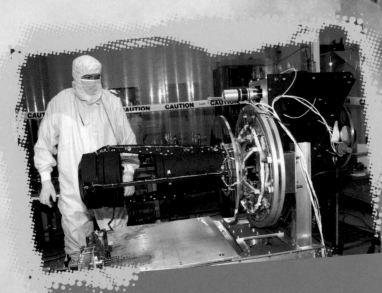

▲ The people who build spacecraft often wear overalls, hoods, gloves, and even masks like surgeons in an operating room.

BUILDING SPACECRAFT

Spacecraft are built in workshops called clean rooms. The rooms have to be completely clean, because dust, oil, and moisture can damage parts of a spacecraft.

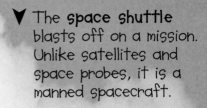

▼ The **space shuttle** blasts off on a mission. Unlike satellites and space probes, it is a manned spacecraft.

Exploring space

Space probes are used to explore the **solar system**. They are sent out into space to photograph planets and their **moons**. They make maps and take lots of measurements for scientists. A few probes have landed on the **Moon** or another planet to study its surface and **atmosphere**.

▼ Some planets are so far away that space probes take years to reach them.

FACT!

The Cassini space probe spent seven years flying from Earth to Saturn.

EARTH SATELLITES

There are about 2,500 satellites flying around Earth. The path of a satellite around a planet is called an orbit. Some satellites circle Earth from north to south, over the North Pole and the South Pole. Other satellites circle the middle of the planet, around the **equator**. Some satellites take exactly one day to fly around the planet. Earth spins once a day too, so these satellites stay above the same spot on the ground all the time.

▲ Communications satellites receive signals from one part of the planet and send them down to another area.

FACT!
On October 6, 1959, Explorer VI was the first satellite to send back a photograph of our planet from space.

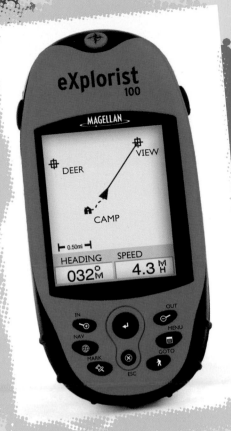

WHERE AM I?

Navigation satellites can tell you exactly where you are on the planet. They are very useful if you are traveling somewhere or if you are lost. The Global Positioning System (GPS) has 24 navigation satellites. A GPS receiver on the ground determines a location by measuring how long it takes for radio signals from the satellites to travel to the receiver.

◀ This little receiver uses radio signals from three GPS satellites in space to determine its position.

Space talk

The American space agency, **NASA**, has its own communications satellites in orbit above Earth. They are called Tracking and Data Relay Satellites (TDRS). The satellites receive signals from NASA, on Earth, and pass them on to spacecraft. The satellites also send signals from the spacecraft back to Earth. This means that NASA can send and receive all the information it needs 24 hours a day.

NASA's Tracking and Data Relay ▶ Satellites send radio signals between spacecraft and their controllers on Earth.

pace probes are unmanned spacecraft sent from Earth to study planets, moons, **comets**, and **asteroids**. Scientists are interested in comets and asteroids because they are made of very old material that has not changed since the solar system began about 4.6 billion years ago. Space probes have flown past, orbited, or landed on nearly every planet in the solar system.

Probing Eros

In 2000, the *NEAR-Shoemaker* space probe went into orbit around an asteroid called 433 Eros. *NEAR-Shoemaker* spent a year studying the asteroid and photographing it from as close as three miles away. Then its controllers on Earth did something the spacecraft wasn't designed to do. They landed the space probe on the asteroid!

▼ The large radio dish in the middle of **NEAR—Shoemaker's solar panels** receives instructions from Earth and sends information back.

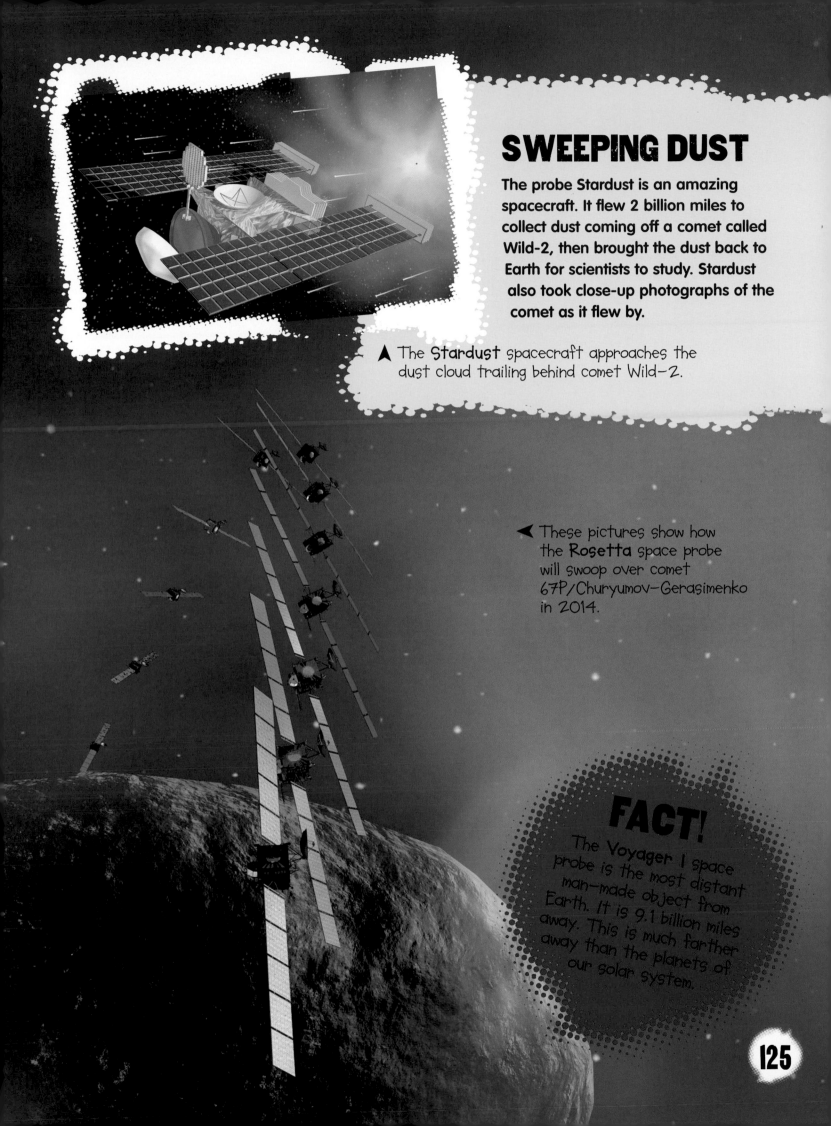

SWEEPING DUST

The probe Stardust is an amazing spacecraft. It flew 2 billion miles to collect dust coming off a comet called Wild-2, then brought the dust back to Earth for scientists to study. Stardust also took close-up photographs of the comet as it flew by.

▲ The **Stardust** spacecraft approaches the dust cloud trailing behind comet Wild-2.

◀ These pictures show how the **Rosetta** space probe will swoop over comet 67P/Churyumov-Gerasimenko in 2014.

FACT!

The Voyager 1 space probe is the most distant man-made object from Earth. It is 9.1 billion miles away. This is much farther away than the planets of our solar system.

125

ORBITERS

Orbiters are space probes that orbit the planets they study. To save fuel during the long journey through space, these probes use the pull of **gravity** of planets they pass to hurl them onward. Then they fire a **rocket** engine to slow down just enough to go into orbit around the planet they have been sent to study. As the space probe circles the planet, its cameras and other instruments study the surface.

Venus Express

On November 9, 2005, the European Space Agency launched a spacecraft called *Venus Express*. It was sent to the planet Venus to study its atmosphere and to find out if volcanoes are still erupting on the planet's surface. The spacecraft's instruments can see right through Venus's thick atmosphere to its surface.

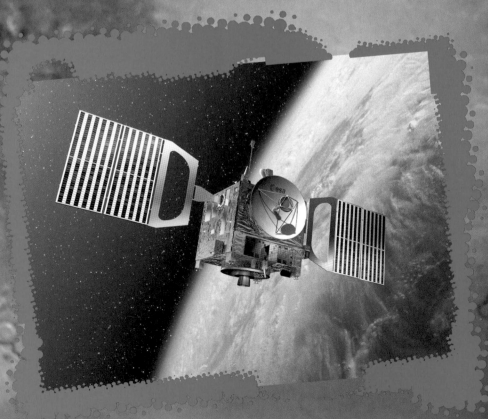

The European **Venus** ➤ **Express** spacecraft went into orbit around Venus on April 11, 2006.

GOING TO SATURN

In 2004, the Cassini spacecraft went into orbit around Saturn. Saturn has huge rings and 56 moons around it. Cassini dropped a small probe called Huygens onto Titan, one of Saturn's moons. Huygens photographed Titan's surface. Scientists are very interested in Titan because, unlike most moons, it has an atmosphere.

Flight mechanics get the huge **Cassini** spacecraft ready for launch. The gold bowl on its side contains the **Huygens** probe. ➤

solar panel

radio dish

◄ In March 2006, seven months after it was launched, the **Mars Reconnaissance Orbiter** began orbiting Mars.

FACT!

Cassini is the biggest spacecraft ever sent to explore a planet and its moons.

SPACE SHUTTLE

The space shuttle is the first manned spacecraft that can be reused. It is made up of a fuel tank and two **boosters**, which carry an orbiter into space. The orbiter has a huge **payload bay** for carrying satellites, space laboratories, and scientific experiments. It spends up to a month in space before it returns to Earth. Five orbiters were built: *Columbia, Challenger, Discovery, Atlantis,* and *Endeavour.*

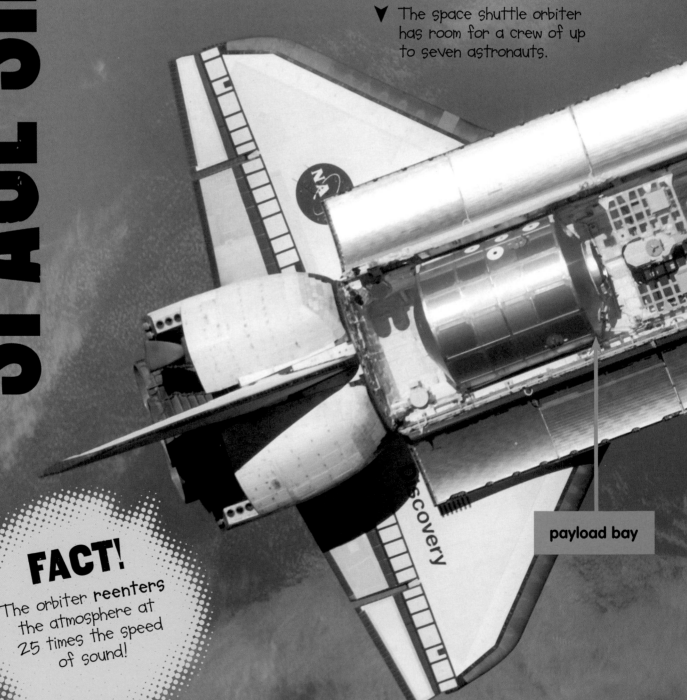

▼ The space shuttle orbiter has room for a crew of up to seven astronauts.

payload bay

FACT!
The orbiter **reenters** the atmosphere at 25 times the speed of sound!

Liftoff

To launch the space shuttle, a huge fuel tank and two **solid rocket boosters** are needed. The tank holds fuel for the three rocket engines in the orbiter's tail. The boosters provide most of the power for liftoff. The fuel tank and boosters fall back to Earth when their job is done.

The space shuttle blasts off. You can see the orange fuel tank, one of the two white solid rocket boosters, and the orbiter. ▶

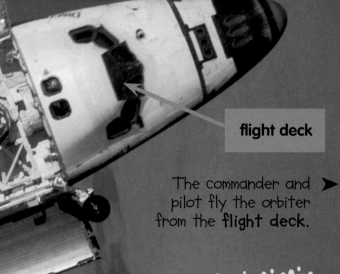

flight deck

The commander and ▶ pilot fly the orbiter from the **flight deck.**

VIRTUAL REALITY

One way for an astronaut to train for a spaceflight is to use virtual reality. Goggles connected to a computer show the astronaut what he will see during a real spaceflight. The astronaut uses special gloves to pick things up and move them around, even though they aren't really there!

◀ Astronauts can train for a space shuttle mission using a virtual reality system. It is similar to a computer game.

129

SOYUZ

Russian Soyuz spacecraft have been carrying people into space since 1967. Today's Soyuz TMA takes astronauts to the **International Space Station**, 250 miles above Earth. The Soyuz TMA has three parts, or **modules**, that link together. The service and orbital modules are at either end of the spacecraft. Between them is the reentry module, which brings the astronauts home.

A Soyuz spacecraft about to **dock** ➤ with the International Space Station.

orbital module

▲ With three astronauts in their bulky spacesuits, there is not much room to spare inside the Soyuz reentry module.

Flying Soyuz

A Soyuz carries three astronauts in its reentry module. They lie back on beds to make liftoff and landing more comfortable. Each bed is covered with a liner that is the same shape as the astronaut's body. The controls for flying the Soyuz are opposite the astronauts.

reentry module

service module

LANDING

At the end of a spaceflight, the reentry module separates from the other two modules. As it falls back into Earth's atmosphere, a heat shield protects the module from the fiery heat of reentry. Then parachutes open and slow it down. Just before the module hits the ground, rockets fire to soften the landing.

▲ The reentry module of a Soyuz spacecraft lies on its side after returning from space.

131

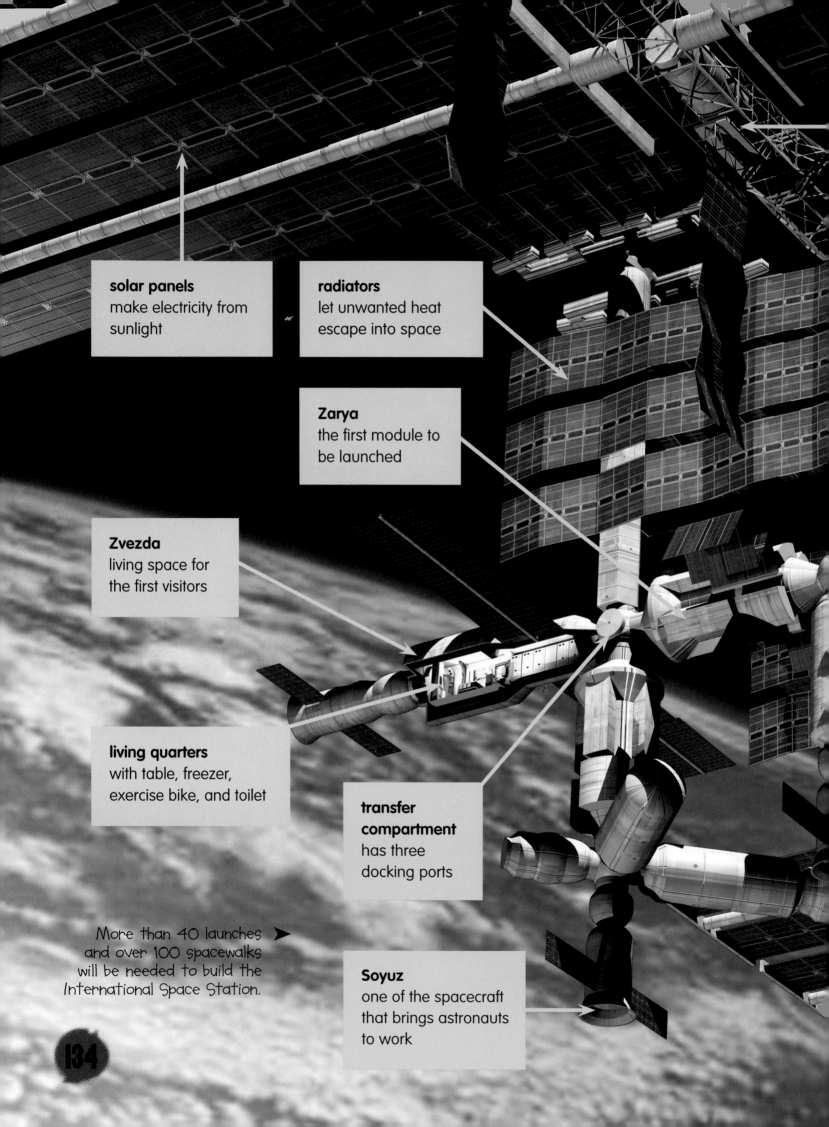

solar panels
make electricity from
sunlight

radiators
let unwanted heat
escape into space

Zarya
the first module to
be launched

Zvezda
living space for
the first visitors

living quarters
with table, freezer,
exercise bike, and toilet

**transfer
compartment**
has three
docking ports

More than 40 launches ➤
and over 100 spacewalks
will be needed to build the
International Space Station.

Soyuz
one of the spacecraft
that brings astronauts
to work

International Space Station

Sixteen countries are working together to build the International Space Station (ISS), about 250 miles above Earth. Like Mir, the ISS is too big and heavy to be launched in one piece. When the ISS is finished, it will measure 360 feet from end to end, and will weigh about 496 tons. It has a laboratory for doing scientific research. A crew of up to seven astronauts will run the station, with the help of 52 computers.

▲ These modules are being built for the International Space Station.

Construction

The parts of the International Space Station that people will live and work in are big metal tubes. They are made from aluminum, which is a very light metal. Connections called **docking ports** allow more modules to connect to the tubes. Visiting spacecraft can "park" at these ports.

Sunrise

Russia started building the ISS when it launched the Zarya (Sunrise) module. Zarya is 41 feet long, 13 feet wide, and weighs 22 tons. It has two rocket engines to boost the space station into a higher orbit, and 36 smaller jets to turn the station.

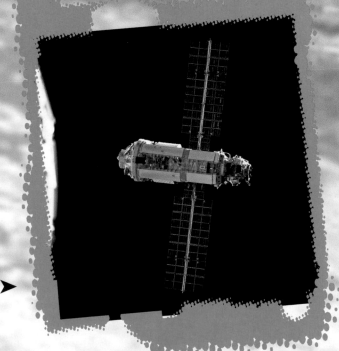

The Zarya module, built in Moscow, ▶ Russia, was launched in 1998.

SPACE STATIONS

Most spacecraft stay in space for a few days or, occasionally, a couple of weeks before returning to Earth. **Space stations** are different. They stay in space for years, and crews take turns running them. The first space stations were used to learn about better ways to build, launch, and run space stations. They also helped scientists find out how astronauts are affected by long space flights. This research will help the scientists design future missions to other planets.

Skylab

The American Skylab space station was made from rockets and spacecraft left over from the Apollo space missions, which landed astronauts on the Moon in the 1960s and 1970s. Skylab crews lived and worked inside part of a giant Saturn V rocket. When Skylab was launched, it was shaken about so badly that one of its solar panels was torn off but, luckily, the space station survived.

▲ Skylab had more room inside than any other spacecraft.

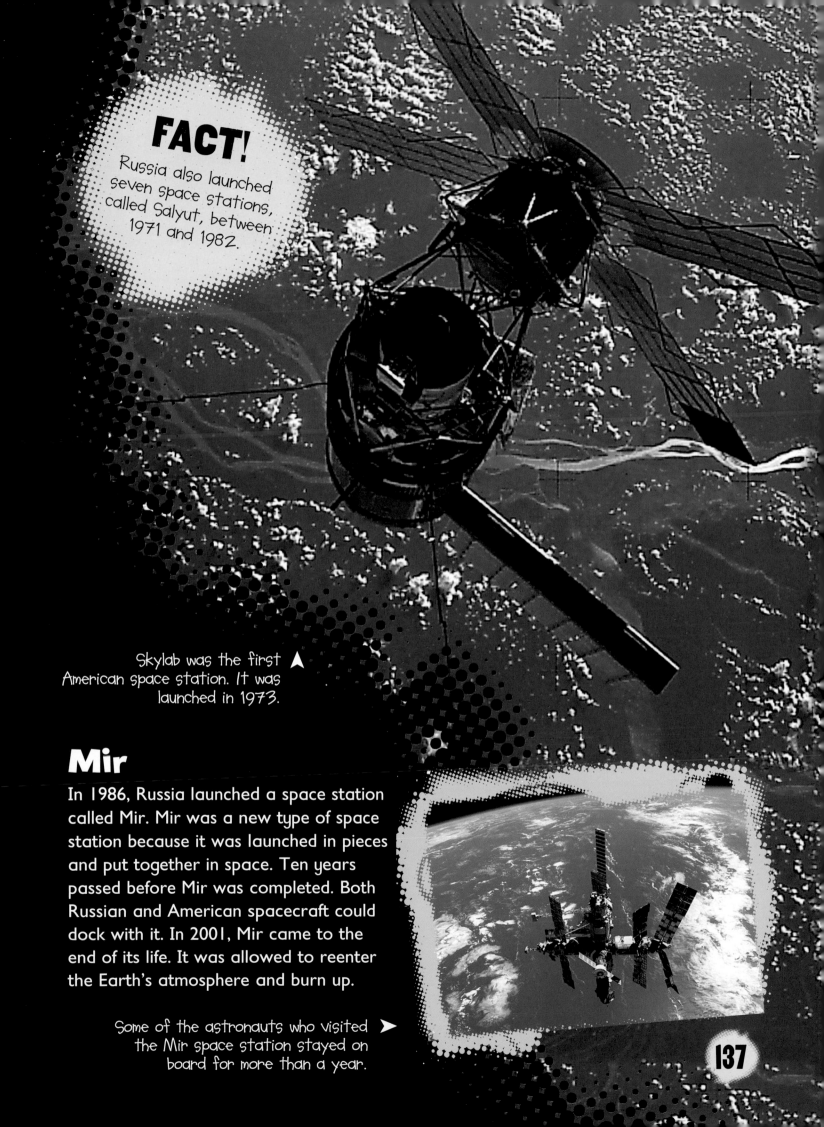

Skylab was the first ▲ American space station. It was launched in 1973.

Mir

In 1986, Russia launched a space station called Mir. Mir was a new type of space station because it was launched in pieces and put together in space. Ten years passed before Mir was completed. Both Russian and American spacecraft could dock with it. In 2001, Mir came to the end of its life. It was allowed to reenter the Earth's atmosphere and burn up.

Some of the astronauts who visited ➤ the Mir space station stayed on board for more than a year.

COLUMBUS

The European Columbus module for the ISS is a science laboratory where astronauts will carry out research. The equipment needed for the experiments will be stored in ten racks. The racks are all the same size and shape, so the equipment for new experiments will slot in easily.

The Columbus orbiting laboratory is being ▲ built by 41 companies in 14 countries.

Delivering cargo

Europe is providing a cargo craft for the ISS, called the Automated Transfer Vehicle (ATV). It is also known as the *Jules Verne*, after an author who wrote many exciting books. The ATV will carry supplies to the space station, but it does not need a crew to fly it. The ATV can find the space station and dock with it automatically.

◀ The Jules Verne cargo craft approaches the ISS.

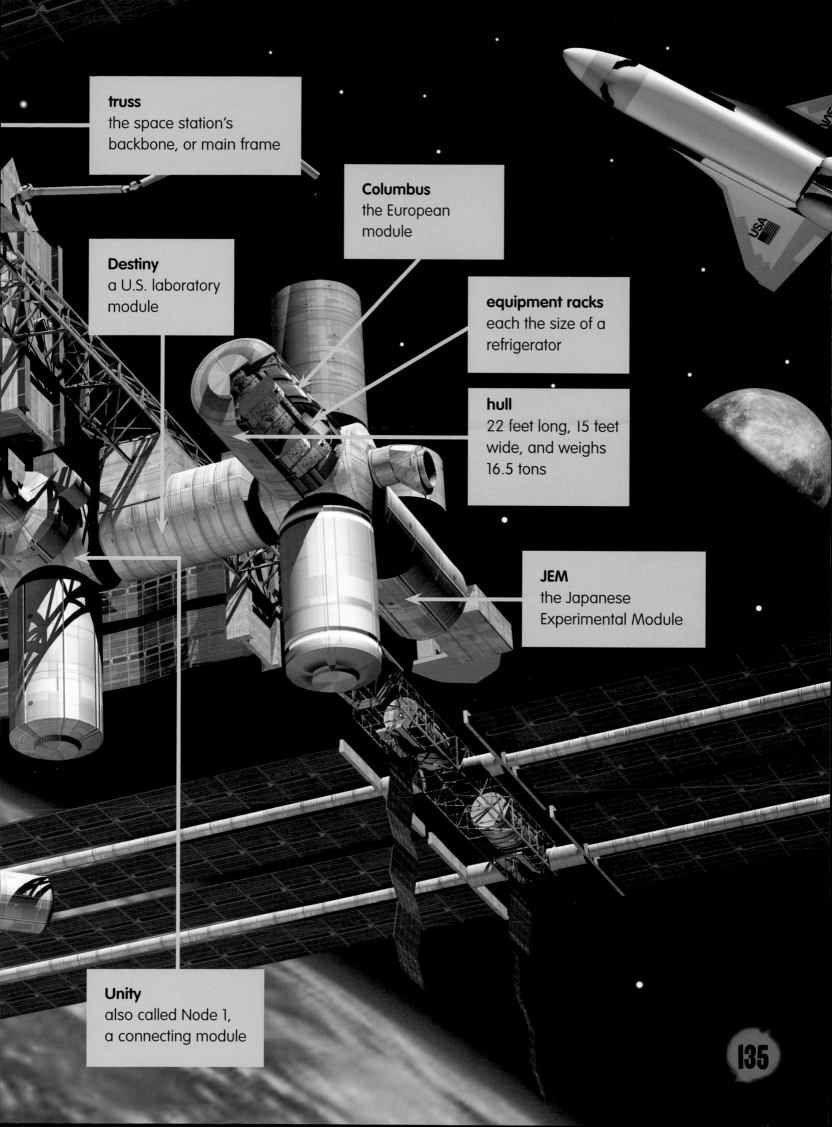

truss
the space station's
backbone, or main frame

Columbus
the European
module

Destiny
a U.S. laboratory
module

equipment racks
each the size of a
refrigerator

hull
22 feet long, 15 feet
wide, and weighs
16.5 tons

JEM
the Japanese
Experimental Module

Unity
also called Node 1,
a connecting module

SPACESUITS

When astronauts have to leave the safety of their spacecraft and go outside, they wear a spacesuit to protect themselves. The spacesuit's backpack has everything the astronaut needs, including oxygen to breathe and radio communication. Astronauts heat up quickly inside their suits when they are working hard. The backpack can pump cool water through one of the spacesuit's layers to cool an astronaut down.

With a spacesuit and a backpack, ➤ an astronaut can work in space for several hours.

SAFER jet pack

▲ Astronauts who drift away can fire their SAFER jet pack to get back to their spacecraft.

A SAFER suit

During spacewalks, astronauts are tied to their spacecraft by a safety line called a tether. This line keeps them from floating away into space. An astronaut also wears a jet pack in case the tether snaps. This jet pack is called a Simplified Aid For **EVA** Rescue (SAFER). Jets of gas from a SAFER pack fly the astronaut back to the spacecraft.

▲ Training for spacewalks is done underwater in one of the world's biggest swimming pools.

MEGAMODELS

Life-size models of parts of the International Space Station and the space shuttle are used to train astronauts for spacewalks. They train underwater wearing their spacesuits, because this feels very similar to being weightless in space.

FACT!

Each space shuttle spacesuit costs about $12.3 million!

ROVERS

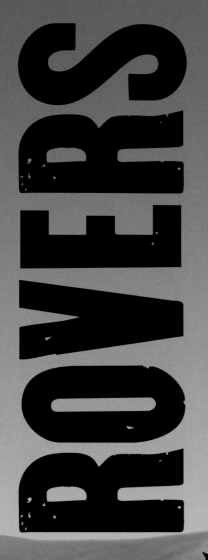

Rovers are robotic space vehicles that land on other planets or moons to explore the surface. They are controlled by drivers on Earth, but sometimes they don't follow orders! Radio signals take so long to travel from Earth to Mars that a rover could crash into a rock long before its driver could steer it to safety. Mars Exploration Rovers have been designed to detect danger and steer around the problem.

➤ Two of these wheelbarrow-sized rovers landed on Mars in 2004.

cameras

radio antenna

instrument arm

FACT!

Mars rovers have heaters to keep them from freezing during the Martian night.

Mars Rovers

In 2004, two Mars Exploration Rovers, called Spirit and Opportunity, were sent to study Mars. On the journey, each rover was folded up inside a **lander** craft. Once on Mars, they unfolded and started exploring the planet's surface. **Solar cells** on top of the rovers made electricity for their motors and instruments. A mechanical arm at the front of each rover stretched out to study nearby rocks.

▲ Technicians check out a Mars Exploration Rover, which is folded up inside the open "petals" of its lander craft.

A Mars lander craft, with its rover safely packed inside, fires rockets to soften its landing. ➤

solar panel

VISITING MARS

After a rover dives into the Martian atmosphere from space, air bags blow up all around it like balloons. A parachute and rockets slow it down as the rover falls toward the surface. When it lands, the rover bounces and rolls to a stop. Then the air bags collapse and the lander craft opens.

ROCKETS

Spacecraft are launched by rockets. Rockets are powerful enough to lift heavy spacecraft and, unlike engines, they work in space. Engines need air to work, but there is no air in space. The biggest rockets are made up of two or three smaller rockets standing on top of each other. These smaller rockets are called **stages**. When each stage has used up all of its fuel, it falls away. This makes the rest of the rocket lighter, so it can fly even faster.

FACT!

▲ Ariane 5 rockets are launched from the European Space Agency's spaceport in French Guiana, in South America.

Ariane 5

Ariane 5, which made its first successful flight in 1997, is Europe's most powerful rocket. It is made from two booster rockets strapped to a two-stage rocket. The boosters provide most of the **thrust** needed to launch the 860-ton rocket into space.

◀ An Ariane 5 rocket stands on the launch pad during the final **countdown** to the launch.

▼ A Proton rocket blasts off. One of these rockets launched the first part of the International Space Station.

Proton

Proton is a Russian rocket with the firepower to launch the heaviest payloads. Space probes weighing more than five tons can be launched to other planets by Proton. It can also take satellites and parts of space stations that weigh up to four times this much into orbit around Earth.

SPACE SCOPES

Scientists learn about **stars** by studying the energy they give out. The swirling air in Earth's atmosphere makes stars twinkle and prevents **telescopes** on Earth from taking clear pictures of them. Stars give out more energy than just light, but Earth's atmosphere blocks a lot of this invisible energy, too. Space telescopes in orbit above the atmosphere receive all the energy given out by stars, and take better pictures.

▲ The Hubble Space Telescope orbits Earth 380 miles above the ground.

FACT!

The Hubble Space Telescope has made more than 400,000 observations of 25,000 objects.

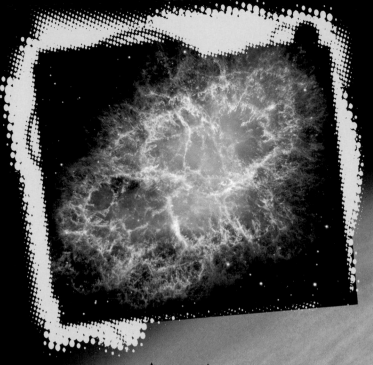

Hubble Space Telescope

The Hubble Space Telescope was launched from a space shuttle in 1990. The Hubble can see objects in space that are 50 times fainter than anything that can be seen by telescopes on Earth. It takes clear pictures and sends them back to Earth by radio.

▲ The Hubble Space Telescope took this picture of the Crab Nebula. This is a star that exploded nearly 1,000 years ago.

▼ The James Webb Space Telescope will see objects that are 400 times fainter than anything that can be seen by telescopes on Earth's surface.

SON OF HUBBLE

The Hubble Space Telescope is nearing the end of its working life. It will be replaced by an even bigger telescope called the James Webb Space Telescope. It is due to be launched in 2013. It will study the birth of new planets, stars, and galaxies.

Heat scope

The Spitzer Space Telescope is an **infrared** telescope. It studies the heat given out by objects in space. This lets it look through clouds of gas and dust and see whatever is hidden inside or behind them. **Astronomers** are interested in these hidden areas of space because this is where new stars form.

◄ The Spitzer Space Telescope makes pictures from heat instead of light.

SPACESHIPONE

Until recently, all spacecraft were launched by space agencies that have government help, such as NASA. The Ansari X Prize offered a reward of $10 million to the first organization to launch a manned spacecraft without any help from the government. To win the prize, the spacecraft had to be launched into space twice within two weeks. Twenty-six teams took part in the race. In 2004, a space plane called *SpaceShipOne* was declared the winner.

At the controls

SpaceShipOne's pilot sits in a cockpit similar to that of an ordinary aircraft. He breathes through a mask, and wears a helmet and a flight suit. He also wears a parachute in case of an emergency.

▲ *SpaceShipOne*'s pilot has a great view of our world from space before the craft begins its return to Earth.

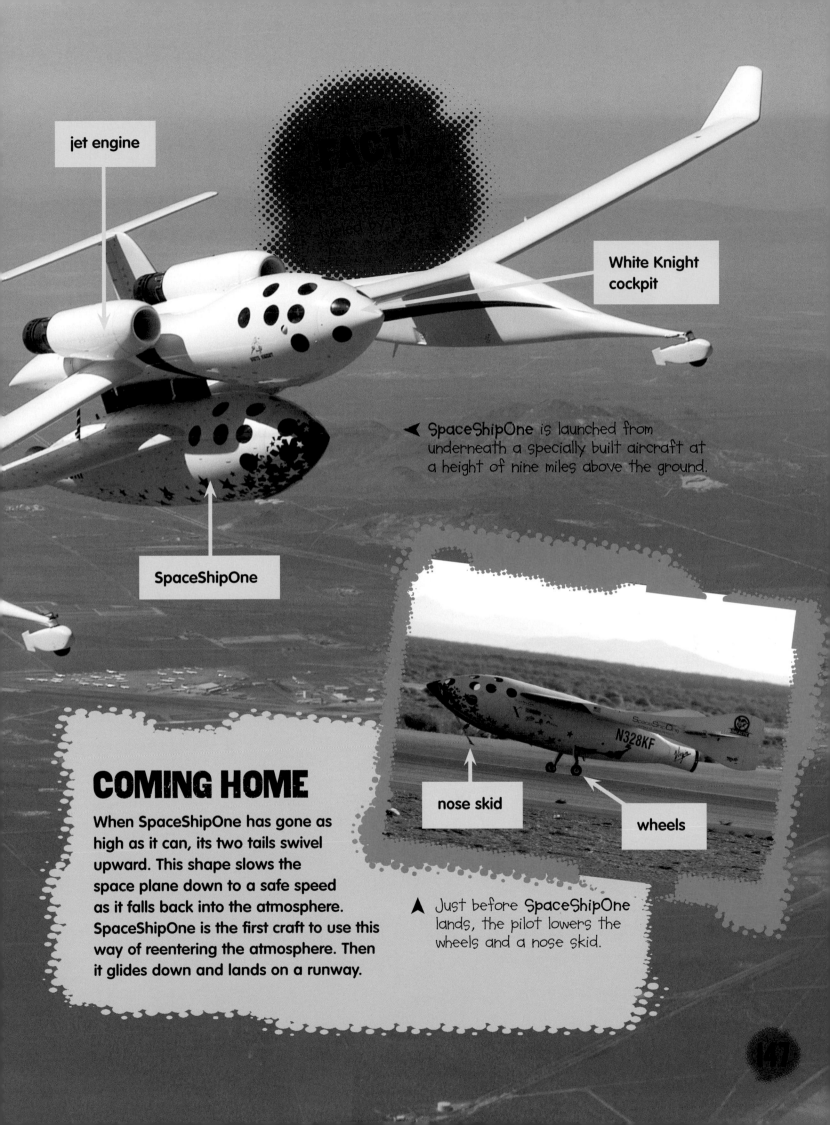

jet engine

White Knight cockpit

SpaceShipOne

◄ SpaceShipOne is launched from underneath a specially built aircraft at a height of nine miles above the ground.

COMING HOME

When SpaceShipOne has gone as high as it can, its two tails swivel upward. This shape slows the space plane down to a safe speed as it falls back into the atmosphere. SpaceShipOne is the first craft to use this way of reentering the atmosphere. Then it glides down and lands on a runway.

nose skid

wheels

N328KF

▲ Just before SpaceShipOne lands, the pilot lowers the wheels and a nose skid.

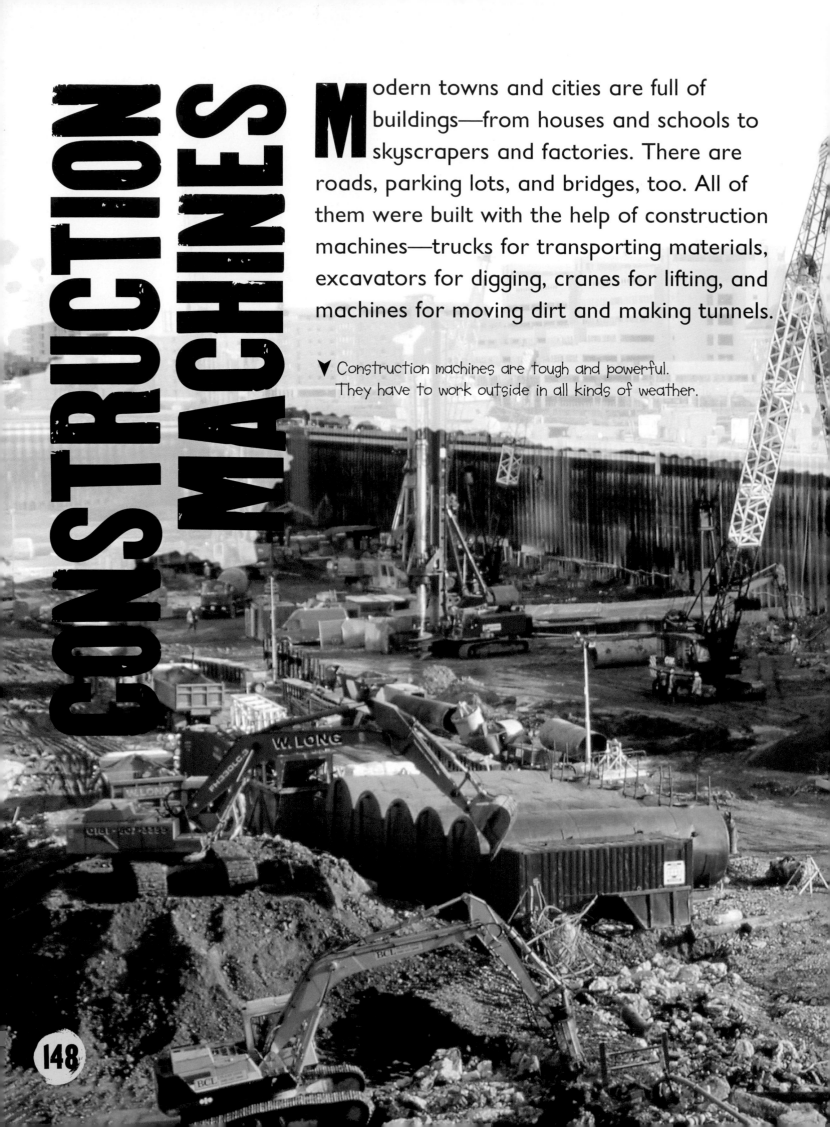

CONSTRUCTION MACHINES

Modern towns and cities are full of buildings—from houses and schools to skyscrapers and factories. There are roads, parking lots, and bridges, too. All of them were built with the help of construction machines—trucks for transporting materials, excavators for digging, cranes for lifting, and machines for moving dirt and making tunnels.

▼ Construction machines are tough and powerful.
   They have to work outside in all kinds of weather.

Machine power

Lots of dirt has to be moved to build modern roads, bridges, and buildings. In the past, large numbers of people did this groundwork, and it took a long time. Today, the power of machines makes it possible to do this type of work in a fraction of the time.

Many modern structures could not be built without construction machines. ➤

THROUGH THE AIR

A big construction site is a jumble of machines, materials, and workers. Everywhere are piles of dirt, sand, and gravel. The quickest way to move heavy materials around the site is to lift them up and carry them through the air. Big construction sites have many cranes for this work.

▲ Tall cranes tower above a construction site.

DIGGERS

Excavators, or diggers, of all sizes are widely used on building sites. They dig holes for the **foundations** of buildings and bridges, as well as trenches for water pipes, **power cables**, and **sewers**. A big **bucket** on the end of a **mechanical arm** digs up the dirt. The arm has joints like your arm, but it is much bigger and stronger.

The bucket at the front of this ➤ huge excavator is designed to scoop up large amounts of dirt and rock.

The seat of this ➤
excavator turns
around to face
the back when the
backhoe is in use.

backhoe

Digging backward

The **backhoe** is one of the most popular digging
machines on construction sites. It has a big, wide
shovel at the front for scooping up earth and
other loose materials. It also has a small bucket,
or backhoe, at the back for digging.

MINI DIGGERS

CONCRETE MIXERS

Huge amounts of concrete are used on a construction site. Concrete is a mixture of sand, gravel, cement, and water. It can be poured, molded, and spread, and it sets rock-hard. Concrete is delivered to construction sites by **concrete mixer trucks**. These have a large drum on top to hold the concrete. The truck's engine slowly turns the drum, and blades inside churn up the mixture.

PUMPING OUT

If the chute at the back of a concrete mixer doesn't stretch to where it is needed on a construction site, a machine called a concrete pump is used. The concrete mixer pours its concrete into a tank at the back of the concrete pump. The pump then forces the concrete out through a long pipe.

◄ A concrete pump carries concrete to exactly where it is needed.

The drum of a concrete mixer must keep turning or the concrete will set hard inside it.

LIEBHERR

HTM 1204

BG·06080

▲ Concrete flows out of the mixer and down a chute onto the ground.

Unloading

To unload concrete, the driver reverses the direction of the drum. The curved blades that mixed the concrete then turn in the opposite direction. This pushes the mixture out of the drum and down a chute at the back of the mixer.

153

DEMOLITION

Old buildings often need to be **demolished** before work on new buildings can begin. Excavators can be equipped with different tools that break up a building piece by piece.

The digging bucket ➤ of this excavator can also be used to pull down walls.

Huge hammers

An excavator's digging bucket can be removed and replaced with other useful demolition tools. In addition to a concrete crusher, it can be equipped with a **hammer**, or breaker. Driven by high-pressure air, the hammer can smash up concrete.

▲ A concrete crusher, or **pulverizer**, can eat through walls like a metal dinosaur!

154

A building that took months to build can be brought down in seconds at the press of a button.

3, 2, 1, BOOM!

Large buildings are demolished by blowing them up. Explosives are placed in the building to blow out the walls and columns that hold it up. The weight of the building then brings down the rest of the structure. The explosives are not set off all at once. They are set off in a carefully planned order so that the building falls down in exactly the right direction and does not damage any other buildings nearby.

EARTH MOVERS

A lot of groundwork has to be done before construction begins on a site. The ground may need to be leveled, and piles of dirt may need to be moved to build roads and bridges. Certain machines are designed to do this hard work. **Bulldozers** push big piles of dirt around, **graders** smooth bumps on rough ground, and **compactors** press down loose dirt with their heavy wheels.

Dump trucks ➤ move dirt around construction sites.

156

FLATTENING EARTH

Bulldozers and scrapers are followed by machines called graders. These are strange-looking vehicles. A grader is like a tractor with a sharp blade underneath. As the grader moves along, the blade scrapes up any bumps of earth and stones that stick up.

▲ Graders smooth the last bumps on the ground and make a flat, even surface.

▼ A bulldozer scrapes up dirt and pushes it to where it is needed.

FACT!

The biggest bulldozer in the world is the Komatsu D575. Its blade is more than 24 feet wide (that's the length of two cars) and over 11 feet high. Bulldozers this big are called superdozers.

TUNNELING MACHINES

In the past, all tunnels were dug by workers using picks and shovels. Explosives were used to blast out solid rock. Today, only the smallest tunnels are dug by hand. The larger tunnels needed for subway trains are dug by giant tunneling machines. These machines have a cutting head at the front covered with sharp metal wheels, or teeth.

A modern tunneling ➤ machine towers over the workers as it is prepared for action.

▲ Rock drills like this are powered by air instead of electricity.

Tiny tunnels

Small tunnels are too narrow for a tunneling machine to fit inside. These tunnels are dug out with the help of air-powered drills, also called **pneumatic drills**. High-pressure air punches the sharp end of the drill into the rock many times each second, chipping the rock away.

FINISHING OFF

Even small tunnels require a hard lining to keep loose rock from falling into the tunnel. First, wire mesh is fastened in place all around the tunnel. Concrete is then sprayed onto it. Finally, long bolts are screwed through the lining into the surrounding rock to hold it in place.

◄ Wire mesh gives the tunnel lining extra strength.

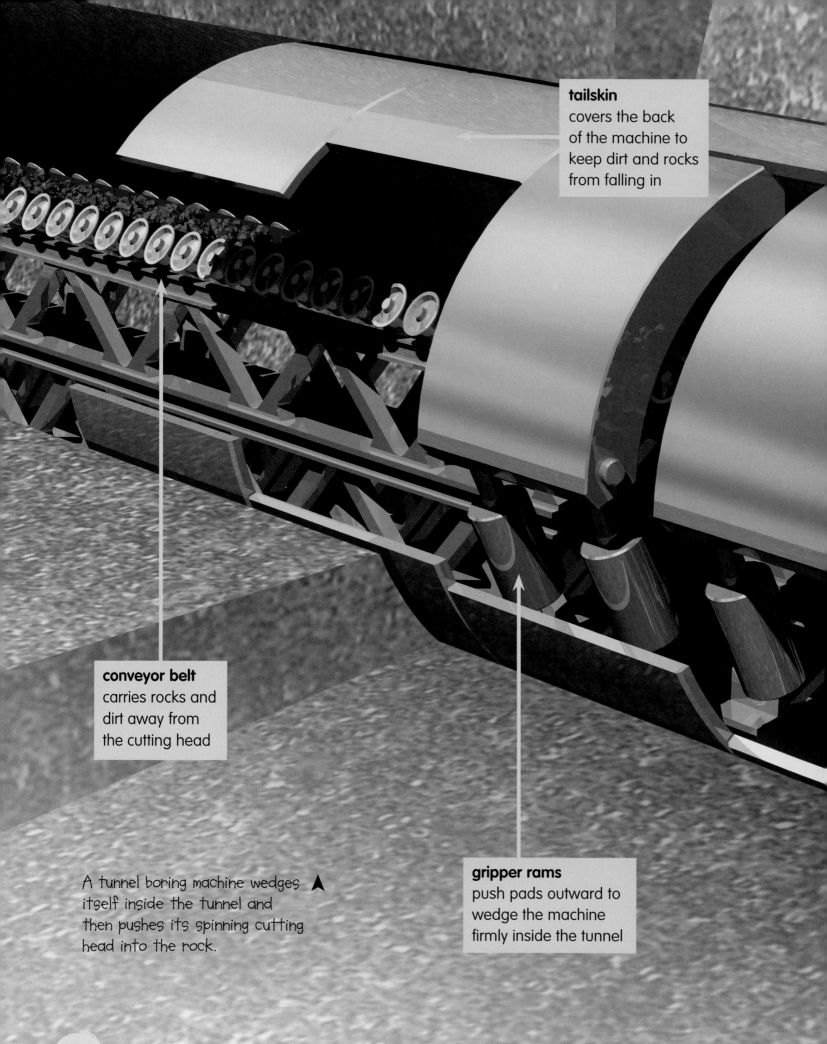

tailskin
covers the back of the machine to keep dirt and rocks from falling in

conveyor belt
carries rocks and dirt away from the cutting head

gripper rams
push pads outward to wedge the machine firmly inside the tunnel

A tunnel boring machine wedges itself inside the tunnel and then pushes its spinning cutting head into the rock.

162

Lining the tunnel

A newly dug tunnel is lined with concrete blocks. They lock together to prevent the tunnel from collapsing. They also provide a smooth, strong surface that heavy equipment can be attached to. Before the tunnel opens, it must be equipped with lights, fans, cameras, and, of course, a road or railroad track. These are all fastened to the concrete lining.

The concrete ► lining ensures that the tunnel is not flattened by the weight of the ground above it.

MECHANICAL MOLES

The longest tunnels are dug by special **tunnel boring machines,** or TBMs. A TBM moves through the ground like a giant mechanical mole, carving out the tunnel as it goes. The machine locks itself in one place inside the tunnel and pushes a cutting head forward to cut through the rock.

The spinning cutting head of the TBM ➤ bites into the rock to carve out the tunnel. The cutting head is covered in dozens of sharp wheels or teethlike cutters called picks. The picks bite into the rock and carve out the tunnel.

Power train

A vehicle called a **service train** travels behind a tunnel boring machine, or TBM, inside the tunnel. An onboard generator makes electricity, which powers the TBM. The service train also removes dirt and rock dug out by the TBM and helps line the tunnel wall.

▲ Rock cut away by the TBM falls onto a moving conveyor belt inside the service train. The rock drops into railroad cars at the end of the train, and the cars take it away.

FACT!
The Channel Tunnel between England and France was built using 11 TBMs. The biggest of them weighed more than 1,500 tons and, together with its service train, measured over 820 feet long—that's the length of 25 buses!

▼ A team of tunnelers stand in front of their road header tunneling machine.

cutting head turns so that the teeth cut into the rock

TUNNEL CUTTER

Tunnels that are too small or too tightly curved for a tunnel boring machine to fit inside may be dug by a machine called a road header. Its cutting head is on the end of a boom that can move up, down, and sideways. The machine's operator steers the boom, and the spinning cutting head cuts rock away to form the tunnel.

◄ The cutting head at the front of a tunnel boring machine turns up to ten times a minute. The speed depends on the hardness of the ground.

thrust rams
push the cutting head
forward and also steer
the machine

cutting teeth
cut into the rock

scraper
scrapes loose rock
away as the cutting
head turns

163

PILES OF WORK

It is very important for a building to stand on firm ground—otherwise it might lean over or even fall down! The famous Leaning Tower of Pisa in Italy leans because its weight squashes the ground more on one side than the other. Modern buildings stand up straight because they are built on top of long "pegs" called **piles** that are driven deep into the ground.

Driving piles into ➤ the ground is one of the first jobs to be done on a construction site.

pile

From the ground up

When the foundations of a big building are finished, rows of steel bars stick out from the tops of the **piles**. A grid of steel bars is then built over the piles. Finally, concrete is poured over all this to lock the base of the building to the piles.

◄ The steel bars that run through concrete are called rebars. This means "reinforcing bars," because the bars reinforce, or strengthen, the concrete.

BORING WORK

Another way to make piles is to bore holes into the ground and then fill them with steel and concrete. A machine called an auger bores holes by drilling into the ground. When the drill is pulled out, the dirt comes out with it. Then the hole is filled in again with concrete and steel.

▲ An auger looks like a giant screw. A motor turns it and drills it into the ground.

167

CRANES

Heavy materials have to be moved around on construction sites. **Tower cranes** are the machines for this job. These cranes have a metal tower with a boom, or arm, balanced on top. The load is lifted by a hook at one end of the boom. The weight of the load is balanced by another heavy weight on the opposite side of the tower.

Traveling cranes

A **mobile crane** is a crane on a truck. Before it lifts anything, legs called **outriggers** come out from its sides and push down onto the ground. These keep the crane level and make it wider so that the load it lifts will not cause it to topple over.

The Millennium Bridge in Gateshead, England, weighs around 850 tons. It was lifted into position by Europe's largest floating crane, the Asian Hercules II.

Hook

Tower cranes ▶ do all the heavy lifting work on construction sites.

FACT!

The world's biggest floating crane is Saipem 7000. It can lift an amazing 14,000 tons!

UNDERWATER LIFTING

If a sunken boat needs to be lifted or a bridge has to be raised into position over a river, a floating crane may be used. This type of crane sits on top of a floating barge.

SUPERHAULERS

Huge amounts of dirt and rock are hauled out of mines and made into cement and other materials used in construction. The hauling work is done by **mine trucks**. These **off-road trucks** never travel on ordinary roads, which means they can be huge. The biggest are called **ultra trucks**.

▲ Ultra trucks are so tall that the driver is less than half the height of one tire!

A GIANT PROBLEM

Ultra trucks are enormous. The cab is so far off the ground that the driver has to climb a ladder to get up to it! Due to the truck's huge size, the drivers can't see behind them. Some trucks have video cameras in the back and screens in the cab so that the driver can see what's behind the truck.

Unloading

Trucks empty out their loads by tipping up the back of the truck so the contents slide onto the ground. The biggest dump trucks can empty out more than 360 tons of dirt in just 30 seconds.

It takes enormous power ➤ to lift the back of a full truck and empty it.

▼ The biggest trucks on earth are used in the mining industry. Some are as big as a house.

ROAD TRUCKS

All kinds of building materials are delivered to construction sites by trucks. Loose materials such as sand, gravel, and dirt are delivered by dump trucks. These are smaller than the giant dump trucks used in mining, because they have to travel on ordinary roads. Many types of goods and materials are transported by different kinds of trucks. Some are **rigid** and others, called **tractor-trailers**, bend in the middle.

A dump truck ➤ transports loose materials such as dirt in a big box that can be tipped up.

Wooden platforms

Heavy items transported by trucks are often carried on wooden platforms called pallets. The pallets have a space underneath so that they can be lifted easily by a forklift.

▲ Forklifts are often used to unload goods from delivery trucks.

ROAD-BUILDING MACHINES

The machines that build roads are called **pavers**. Small stones and a thick, black, oily substance called **asphalt**, or **blacktop**, are loaded into a paver. The machine mixes the stones and hot asphalt together. As it moves along slowly, the paver spreads the mixture on the ground to make a new road.

A paver spreads ▲ steaming hot asphalt mixed with small stones onto the ground.

A machine called a **roller** follows the paver. As ➤ it drives up and down the road, its heavy rollers flatten and harden the newly laid road surface.

FARM MACHINES

In the past, people who grew crops and raised animals had few machines to help them. The hard work of pulling heavy **plows** and wagons was done by horses or **oxen**. These days, farming is completely different. In many countries, horses and oxen have been replaced by **tractors** and other farm machines. This means that big farms can be run by fewer people—and can produce more food than ever.

Space-age farming

Today, the most advanced farm machines use computers. Computers can give information about how much plant food a crop needs, how wet the soil is, and how well crops are growing. Farmers can even track a machine's exact position on a farm by using radio signals from **satellites**.

◄ Farmers use computer and satellite equipment in their tractors to help them produce bigger and better crops.

▼ Long, curved knives called scythes were once used to cut wheat and grass by hand. On modern farms, machines called **combines** bring in the wheat crop in a fraction of the time.

tractor

manure spreader

corn harvester

combine

TYPES OF FARM MACHINES

There are all kinds of machines in use on farms today. Tractors pull plows and other machines that work the soil, combines and corn harvesters bring in the crops, and cutting machines mow grass and trim hedges.

▲ Farm machines come in all shapes and sizes. Each machine is designed to do a specific job.

TRACTORS

Tractors are probably the most useful of all farm machines. A tractor has big **grooved** tires that can grip soft, muddy ground. A powerful engine helps the tractor pull heavily loaded **trailers** or drag plows behind it through the soil. The driver sits high up in the cab. Big windows give him a clear view all around.

exhaust pipe

diesel engine

driver's cab

splash guard

grooved tires

FASTRAC

3220

FACT!
The **power takeoff** lets a tractor's engine power another machine, such as a grass cutter, towed by the tractor. It was invented in 1922.

▲ Most farm jobs are done by tractors, which is why they are called the workhorses of modern farms.

SPECIAL VEHICLES

Tractors do most of the heavy work on farms, but other vehicles are needed for some jobs. Loaders pile up bales of hay and straw.

◄ Even a small loader can lift heavy bales.

Power to spare

Plows are machines that can be attached to tractors and used to turn over the soil. Special arms at the back of the tractor can lift the plow clear of the ground when it is not in use.

plow

A tractor can raise ► and lower a plow.

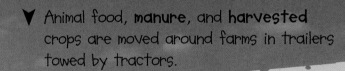

▼ Animal food, **manure**, and **harvested** crops are moved around farms in trailers towed by tractors.

CROSS-COUNTRY

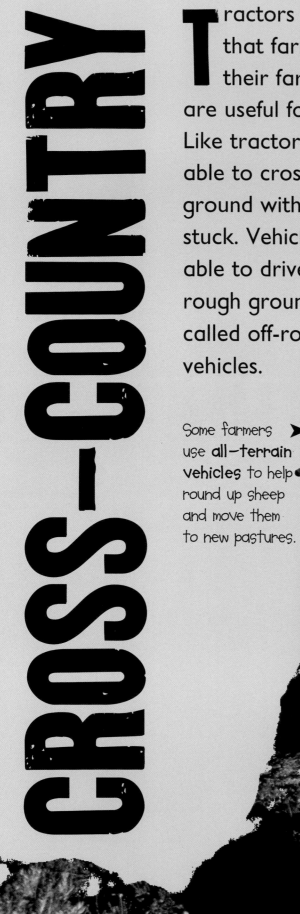

Tractors are not the only vehicles that farmers use to get around their farms. All kinds of vehicles are useful for driving across farmland. Like tractors, they must be able to cross soft or soggy ground without getting stuck. Vehicles that are able to drive across rough ground are called off-road vehicles.

Some farmers ➤ use **all-terrain vehicles** to help round up sheep and move them to new pastures.

FLYING FARMERS

Not all farm vehicles work on the ground. Aircraft are sometimes used for farmwork, especially on big farms and cattle ranches in the United States, Canada, and Australia. Helicopters are sometimes used to round up cattle and horses on large ranches. The wind from the spinning rotor blades and the noise of the helicopter drive the animals away from it.

▼ A helicopter hovers close to the ground to drive cattle ahead of it.

Four-wheel drive

Ordinary cars do not work well on farms—they get stuck easily on muddy ground. This is because only two of their four wheels are driven by the engine. In an off-road vehicle, all four wheels are powered by the engine. This helps the tires grip muddy or wet ground.

◄ Four-wheel-drive off-road vehicles can travel around farmland almost as well as tractors.

Before crops can be planted, the ground must be prepared. The soil surface is broken up to let in air and water. Stirring up the soil also helps kill weeds. This heavy work is done by machines. Plows turn over the soil, and **harrows** break it up. Then **cultivators** and **rakes** make a flat, even surface ready for planting seeds.

Plows have a set of curved ▶ blades that slice through the soil and turn it over.

▲ A harrow breaks up big clumps of soil.

Harrows

Harrows are dragged by tractors across plowed soil to level out the humps and hollows made by the plow. They have **disks**, teeth, or spikes to cut through the earth. Harrows are also useful for flattening molehills.

SPREADING WASTE

Animal waste, also called manure, contains natural plant food that helps grass and crops to grow. It is collected from the farmyard and laid on the ground by a machine called a manure spreader.

▲ As a tractor drives along, a manure spreader lays manure behind it.

PLANTING MACHINES

Once the soil has been prepared, the next job is to plant the crops. It would take too long to plant seeds by hand, so today farmers use machines. Not all seeds planted in open ground grow into healthy plants, however. Many are eaten by birds or killed by bad weather or disease. Some crops are planted in greenhouses or plastic tunnels, where they can grow in safer conditions. When they have become small plants, or **seedlings**, they are moved out to the fields.

▲ Potato plants are grown from small potatoes called seed potatoes. A potato-planting machine pushes the potatoes into piles of soil called ridges.

SOWING SEEDS

A seed-sowing machine cuts a narrow trench, **or slit, in the soil and then drops seeds into it. The machine plants the seeds in rows. The space left between the rows allows room for machines to come along later and harvest the crop.**

seed drill

◄ The machine that plants seeds is called a seed drill.

Planting seedlings

Seedlings are easily damaged and have to be handled carefully. The machines that plant seedlings are called **transplanters**. They have a pair of soft plastic grippers for picking up each seedling. Transplanters make a hole in the ground and then push the seedling into it.

◄ This machine is covering the ground with a thin plastic layer. The plastic cover warms the soil, keeps it moist, and stops weeds from growing. Seedlings are planted through holes in the cover.

TAKING CARE OF CROPS

As crops grow, the young plants must be fed and watered. Plant food, called **fertilizer**, is sprinkled on the soil. Farmers must also make sure the plants have enough water, so if there is not enough rain, the crops have to be watered. Supplying farmland with extra water is called **irrigation**. Chemicals may be sprayed onto crops to kill insects and other pests that might harm them. **Organic** farms raise crops and animals without using **artificial** chemicals.

Aerial work

One way of spraying crops is to do it from the air, using airplanes or helicopters. Liquid is stored in tanks inside the aircraft and sprayed out of pipes over the crops. The aircraft that do this work are called crop dusters.

◄ A crop duster swoops low over the crops to spray its chemicals onto the plants.

▼ A fertilizer spreader drops small pellets of fertilizer from a tank called a hopper onto a spinning disk or spout. This throws the pellets out onto the ground.

hopper

WIND AND WATER

On some farms, windmills are used for pumping water up from underground or for collecting crops. The wind turns blades that drive the water pump.

187

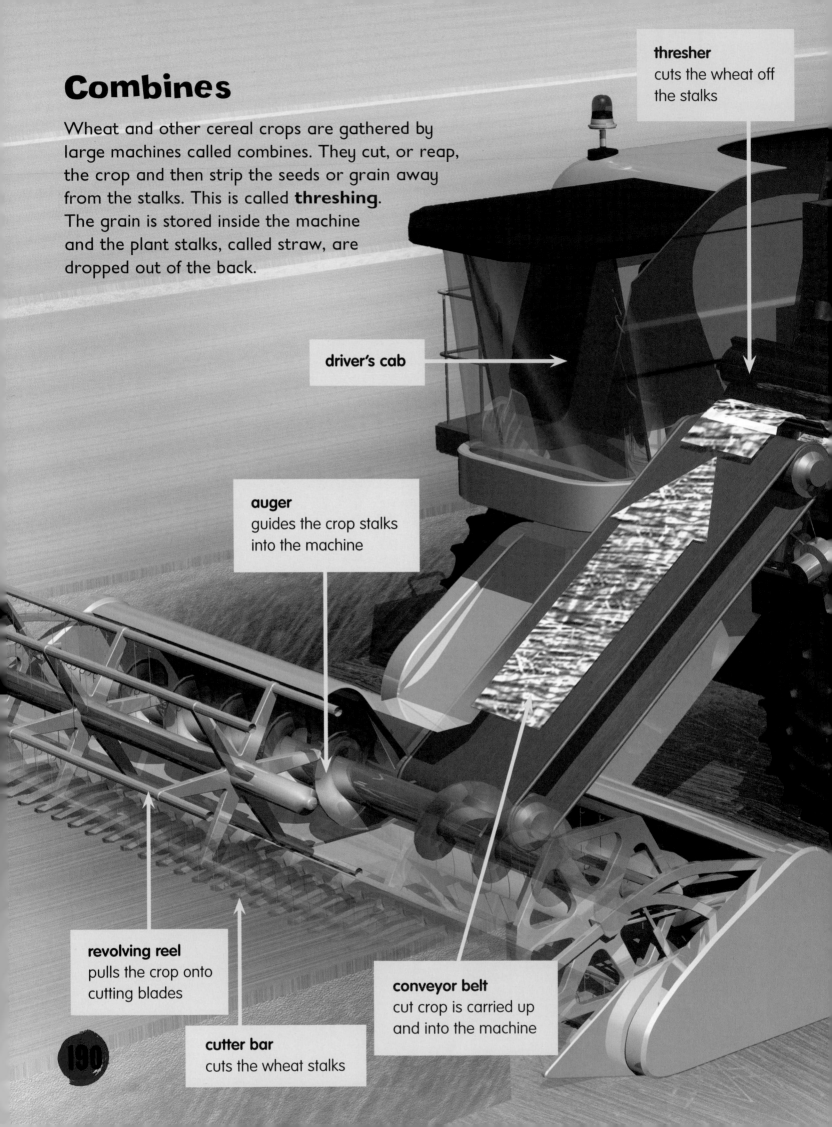

Combines

Wheat and other cereal crops are gathered by large machines called combines. They cut, or reap, the crop and then strip the seeds or grain away from the stalks. This is called **threshing**. The grain is stored inside the machine and the plant stalks, called straw, are dropped out of the back.

thresher
cuts the wheat off the stalks

driver's cab

auger
guides the crop stalks into the machine

revolving reel
pulls the crop onto cutting blades

conveyor belt
cut crop is carried up and into the machine

cutter bar
cuts the wheat stalks

190

Floating ➤ harvesters cut and collect underwater weeds to prevent them from choking the waterways.

COTTON HARVESTERS

Cotton is a crop that is grown in huge quantities and made into clothes. Its fibers grow on the seeds of the cotton plant, which are harvested by machines. Some farmers remove the whole seed pod with the cotton fibers still inside, but others take just the cotton fibers.

When tufts of ➤ white fibers burst out of the seed pods of cotton plants, it is time to harvest the crop.

HARVESTING

When a crop is fully grown, it must be gathered, or **harvested**. Different types of crops are harvested in different ways. The most valuable part of a grain crop is the seeds. In root crops, such as carrots or potatoes, the roots hidden underground are harvested. The most important part of crops such as oranges and grapes is the fruit. Some crops are still harvested by hand, but machines are used wherever possible.

MAKING BALES

Baling machines **collect hay or straw and press it into cylindrical or box-shaped bundles called bales. Bound with ties, bales can be moved and stored more easily than loose hay and straw.**

The baler behind this tractor ▲ picks up straw and rolls it up into cylindrical bales.

Collecting grass

Grass is gathered by a machine called a **forage harvester**. It picks up the cut grass off the ground and blows it through a long, curved spout into a trailer that is driven alongside the harvester.

▲ A forage harvester collects grass that will be made into hay.

▲ Harvesttime is the busiest time of the year on a farm. Machines help farmers harvest their crops quickly.

193

Grapes, olives, ▶
blueberries, and
raspberries can
be picked by a
harvesting machine.
This machine shakes
the fruit free from
trees and bushes and
catches it as it falls.

Hay and straw

Mown grass and plant stalks
left behind by a combine are
not gathered immediately.
They are left on the ground
to dry out for a while. Then
they are pushed into long
piles called **windrows** by
rakes or by machines called
swathers.

◀ The spiked wheels of
this farm rake are
brushing mown grass
into windrows.

beater
separates the grain
from the unwanted
husks (seed coats)

grain elevator
unloads grain into
a truck or trailer

FACT!
In the 1930s, the first
combine to be driven
by an engine was built.
Before then, all combines
were pulled by horses.

grain sieve
the grain falls through
the sieve into a box

▲ A combine separates the grain from
wheat plants, keeps the grain, and
drops the rest on the ground.

CUTTERS

Farms sometimes have long hedges that have to be cut back regularly to prevent them from growing too big. Tall hedges cast long shadows that keep light from reaching nearby plants. Wide hedges take up space in which crops could grow. Ordinary hedges around a lawn can be cut with handheld trimmers, but farm hedges are bigger and longer and must be cut with bigger machines.

Power Arm 95

blades

▲ A mowing machine has razor-sharp blades for cutting grass.

GRASS CUTTING

Grass is an important food for farm animals. During the summer, the animals eat lush, fresh grass in the fields. Grass does not grow in the winter, so cattle and sheep are given hay to eat instead. Hay is long grass that is cut and dried in the summer. Green plants can also be cut and stored to make a food called silage. Grass is cut by machines called mowers.

Trimming trees

Trees are cut down with chainsaws. A small motor drives a metal chain around the edge of a long, flat metal blade. The fast-moving chain has sharp teeth that cut through the wood.

A chainsaw can cut ▶ through thick branches and tree trunks quickly and easily.

◀ A hedge—cutting machine on the end of a tractor's mechanical arm is used to keep farm hedges neatly trimmed.

LIFTERS

Lifting hay bales and other heavy materials is hard work, which is why farmers use machines to do the job. Some tractors can have a big, wide bucket, called a **loader** bucket, attached to the front. This is useful for scooping things up off the ground. The **telehandler** is a different kind of lifting machine. Its name means "telescopic handler." It uses a long arm, or **boom**, to lift things.

A telehandler's ➤ boom is a useful tool. It can reach forward and lift things.

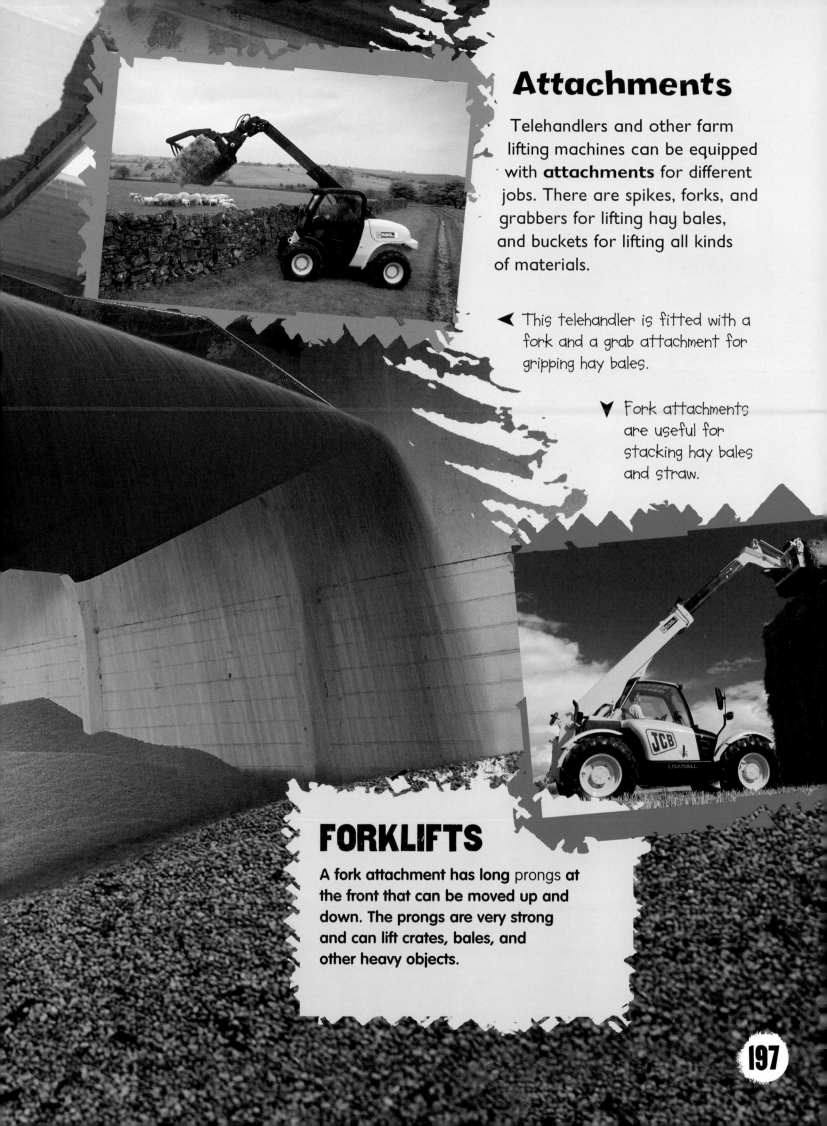

Attachments

Telehandlers and other farm lifting machines can be equipped with **attachments** for different jobs. There are spikes, forks, and grabbers for lifting hay bales, and buckets for lifting all kinds of materials.

◄ This telehandler is fitted with a fork and a grab attachment for gripping hay bales.

▼ Fork attachments are useful for stacking hay bales and straw.

FORKLIFTS

A fork attachment has long prongs at the front that can be moved up and down. The prongs are very strong and can lift crates, bales, and other heavy objects.

TAKING CARE OF ANIMALS

Most of the machines used on farms with animals are the same tractors, trailers, loaders, and **excavators** that are used on crop farms. However, there are a few machines that are specially designed for taking care of animals, such as milking machines. At one time, cows were milked by hand, which was a long, slow process. Today, cows are milked by machines that mimic the sucking action of calves.

Milking machines

Before milking begins, the cow's **udder** is washed. All the milk collected from the cow is pumped into a tank and chilled to keep it fresh.

Four tubes, called a cluster, gently ▶ suck milk out of each cow's udder in the same way a feeding calf would.

▲ An experienced shearer can shear up to 17 pounds of wool from a sheep in less than two minutes.

SHEARING

Sheep have their wool shorn, or cut off, at least once a year. Powered clippers are used for the job. A motor slides the blades across each other about 3,000 times a second!

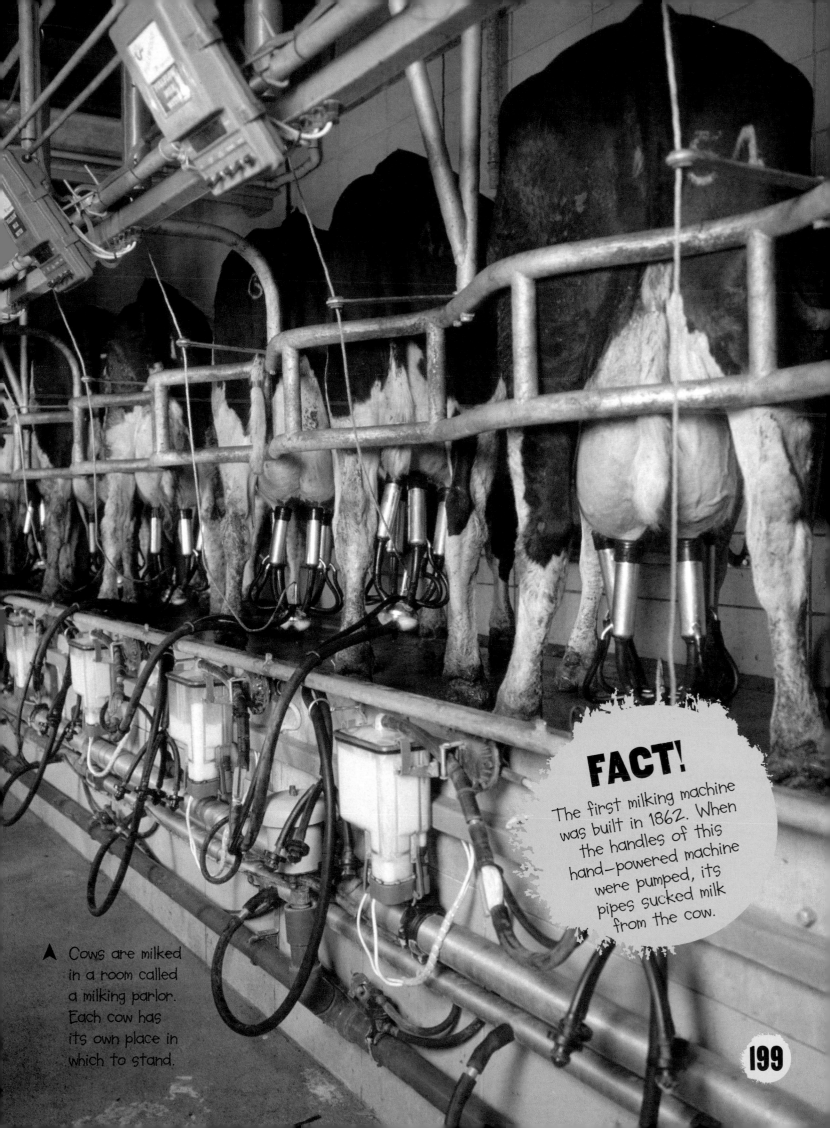

FACT!

The first milking machine was built in 1862. When the handles of this hand-powered machine were pumped, its pipes sucked milk from the cow.

▲ Cows are milked in a room called a milking parlor. Each cow has its own place in which to stand.

DIGGERS

Holes are dug on farms by many different types of machines. Lots of them are the same as machines used on construction sites. They have a mechanical arm with a bucket on the end. The arm pushes the bucket into the ground. Teeth along the edge of the bucket help break up the dirt and scoop it up. There are even machines that make holes for fence posts and trenches for sewers.

The **backhoe** is a digging ➤ machine. It has a small bucket at the back for digging and a wide bucket at the front for scooping and loading.

Post work

Machines are also used on farms to put up fences. **Posthole augers** drill holes into the ground to hold fence posts. If the ground is not too hard, machines called **post drivers** can hammer the posts straight into the ground.

▲ A posthole auger is screwed into the ground and pulled out again to make a neat hole for a fence post.

DIGGING DITCHES

Soggy soil is bad for plants because it rots their roots. One way to dry out wet land is to dig narrow slots with trenching machines and clay drains at the bottom. Another way is to use a machine called a mole plow, which cuts channels under the ground for water to drain into.

◄ A trenching machine slices through the ground and makes a long, narrow channel through which water can drain away.

201

TRUCKS

A lot of heavy materials have to be transported to and from farms. Supplies such as fertilizer and animal food are delivered, and harvested crops are taken away for sale. Milk must be collected from dairy farms every day, and animals such as cattle and sheep also need to be transported. Some of the biggest trucks on the roads do this work.

Milk tank trucks are made ➤ from stainless steel because it will not rust and spoil the milk.

A moving belt loader fills a truck with harvested potatoes. The top end of the belt can be moved up or down to the right height for the truck. ➤

Dump trucks

Many of the trucks that do the heavy moving in the farming industry are dump trucks. They are filled up by a machine called a loader, or by a conveyor belt. Then, to empty its load, the back of the truck tips up and everything inside slides out.

◄ Dump trucks collect all kinds of harvested crops from farms.

203

EMERGENCY MACHINES

When accidents happen or disaster strikes, emergency vehicles rush to the rescue with well-trained crews. There are many different types of emergency vehicles, from motorcycles, cars, vans, and trucks to helicopters, airplanes, boats, ships, and even submarines. Most carry special equipment and supplies at all times—there is never time to pack when an emergency call comes in!

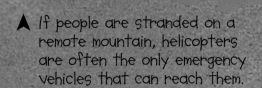
▲ If people are stranded on a remote mountain, helicopters are often the only emergency vehicles that can reach them.

MACHINE POWER

Emergency vehicles are equipped with lots of special machines. Fire trucks have pumps that spray hundreds of gallons of water over fires. They also carry powerful cutting tools to release people trapped inside cars or buildings. Firefighting airplanes have big water tanks that can be emptied over a fire in a matter of seconds.

◄ Fire trucks are packed with extra tools, hoses, and supplies.

◄ Different types of emergency vehicles and their crews work together to deal with major accidents and emergencies.

LIFEBOATS

Lifeboats are emergency vehicles that rescue people in danger on the open water. Some lifeboats are carried aboard larger ships. The crew and passengers use them to escape in an emergency. Other lifeboats are sent out from land to rescue people who are in trouble out at sea. Some lifeboats are self-righting, which means that even if waves push them over, they can turn themselves the right way up again.

▲ Even in terrible weather, lifeboats and their crews go out to save lives.

SURF RESCUE

Small inflatable **boats rescue people in shallow waters near the shore. These boats have flat bases and are made from a rubber tube filled with air. Rigid inflatable boats, also called RIBs, rescue people farther from the shore. RIBs have a hard plastic** hull **with a rubber tube around the top.**

◄ Surf rescue boats go to the aid of people in the water near the shore.

Offshore emergency

Giant platforms in the sea drill for oil and natural gas under the ocean floor. They have their own lifeboats, which workers use in an emergency. Each of these lifeboats is sealed shut so that it will float in even the roughest of seas!

FACT!
The first lifeboat was designed and built in the 1780s by an Englishman named Lionel Lukin.

▲ The survival boats of oil-rig platforms are completely watertight to protect the passengers inside.

207

AIR RESCUE

The fastest way to find and rescue people in remote places is to use aircraft. Helicopters are ideal for rescue work because they can **hover** over one spot and can land almost anywhere. Airplanes cannot hover like helicopters and they need runways to land on. However, they can fly faster than helicopters and can search large areas more quickly. They can also carry out rescue flights over long distances.

▲ Search-and-rescue helicopters can lift people to safety using a machine called a **winch**.

▼ Sea King helicopters take part in all kinds of rescues on mountains, in remote areas, and at sea.

KING OF THE SEA

The Sea King is one of the most widely used search-and-rescue helicopters. It is a big aircraft with rotor blades that are 62 feet across—that's the length of more than six cars! It can weigh almost 11 tons and carry more than 20 people, or nine stretchers and a few doctors.

UNDERWATER EMERGENCIES

Underwater emergency vehicles rescue sailors trapped in sunken submarines. Some of these emergency machines are **submersibles**, and others are **diving bells** that are lowered on the end of a long cable. Remotely operated vehicles, or **ROVs**, are also used in submarine rescues. An ROV does not have a crew. It is "driven" by an operator in a nearby ship and has gripping and cutting tools to free a trapped submersible.

▼ The LR5 rescue sub has a crew of three—a pilot, copilot, and systems officer.

Rescue sub

The LR5 rescue sub can dive to about 1,300 feet and rescue 15 people at a time. It lands on top of the escape hatch of a sunken submarine. The trapped sailors can then climb up to safety through the hatch and into the rescue vehicle.

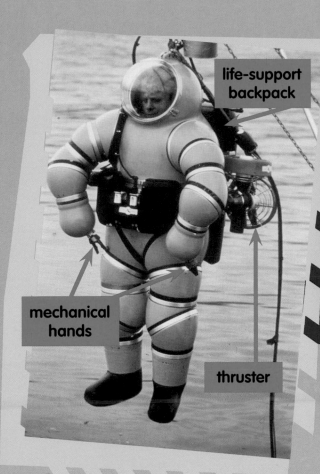

life-support backpack

mechanical hands

thruster

HARD SUIT

A strong, rigid metal suit called a "hard suit" can withstand the pressure of deep water. Divers wear hard suits when diving in very deep water. The suit has its own propellers, or thrusters, at the back to move it around through the water. It looks a little bit like a space suit!

◀ Divers can wear hard suits to reach sunken submersibles so that they can help with the rescue operation.

▲ The U.S. Navy's Deep Submergence Rescue Vehicle (DSRV) can dive to a depth of over 4,000 feet.

POLICE VEHICLES

The police are often the first people to arrive at emergencies of different kinds. Police officers travel in cars packed with computer and radio equipment. Police cars are also called cruisers, squad cars, or patrol cars. Most are brightly painted so everyone can see them, but some look like regular cars so that officers can travel around without being noticed.

▲ Police cars like this Ford Crown Victoria are ordinary cars that have been strengthened and improved especially for police work.

◄ Police departments use trained dogs to search for missing people. The dogs are carried in special vans with a cage in the back.

Police technology

Most police cars now have a laptop computer inside. This means officers can look up information about people and other cars when they are out on the road. Some cars have a video camera and a **radar** system for checking the speed of other vehicles.

◄ Police officers keep in touch with each other by radio. Their cars may also have computer, video, and radar equipment to help them catch people who break the law.

Police boats are used for dealing with emergencies on the water. ►

AIR FORCE

Police helicopters allow officers to search the ground faster than officers on foot. They can often spot escaping criminals from the air. Their cameras record pictures of events on the ground, such as car chases. At night they can light up the ground with powerful lights or use thermal cameras that can "see" in the dark.

◄ Police helicopters like this Eurocopter EC–135 are used to track criminals in cars or on foot.

213

AMBULANCES

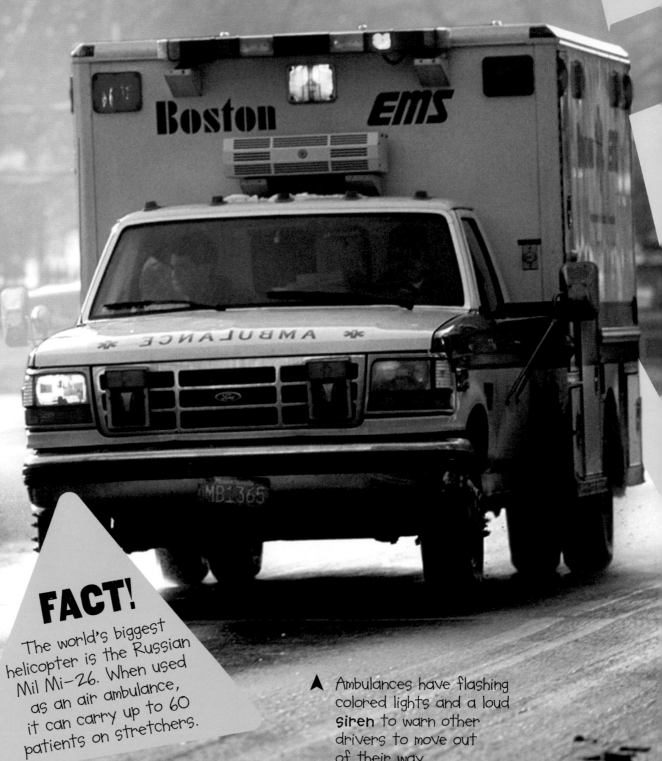

Ambulances are packed with medical equipment. This means that the crew can treat people on the way to the hospital. There is room inside for patients who need to lie on stretchers. They are cared for by people called paramedics, who are trained to give emergency medical help.

FACT!

The world's biggest helicopter is the Russian Mil Mi-26. When used as an air ambulance, it can carry up to 60 patients on stretchers.

▲ Ambulances have flashing colored lights and a loud **siren** to warn other drivers to move out of their way.

Air ambulances

Some people are so ill or badly hurt that they have to be moved quickly to the hospital by air. An **air ambulance** is a helicopter that can carry patients to the hospital much faster than a road ambulance.

Air ambulances have space for ➤ sick or injured people on stretchers. They also carry medical equipment so that the crew can care for patients during the flight.

FLYING DOCTORS

Australia is a big country, and many people there live far away from the hospitals in towns and cities. In these places, emergency medical help is provided by the Royal Flying Doctor Service. Each day, its aircraft fly more than 30,000 miles and its doctors help more than 500 people.

◄ The Royal Flying Doctor Service's aircraft have been helping people in remote parts of Australia since 1928.

The cabin of an air ➤ ambulance plane has beds and lots of medical equipment. It looks like a small hospital.

215

ladder
can extend
to a height of
98 feet

rams
lengthen to
raise the ladder

water pipe
carries water up the ladder

high-pressure oil
makes the ram extend
with great force

A fire truck's ladder ➤
has many sections that
slide inside each other.

lockers
contain extra tools
and equipment

218

FIRE BOATS

Fire boats are firefighting vessels that deal with fires on ships. They suck in seawater and pump it out over the fire. Each boat has several nozzles so that water can be directed onto different parts of a burning ship.

Seawater is pumped out of a fire ➤ boat with such force that it can reach more than 30 feet in the air!

FACT!

The world's most powerful fire boat is the Los Angeles Fire Department's Fireboat number 2. The 105-foot-long boat can pump over 38,300 gallons of water every minute.

◀ Firefighters going into smoke-filled buildings wear a special mask to keep out smoke and fire. They also breathe air from tanks on their backs.

217

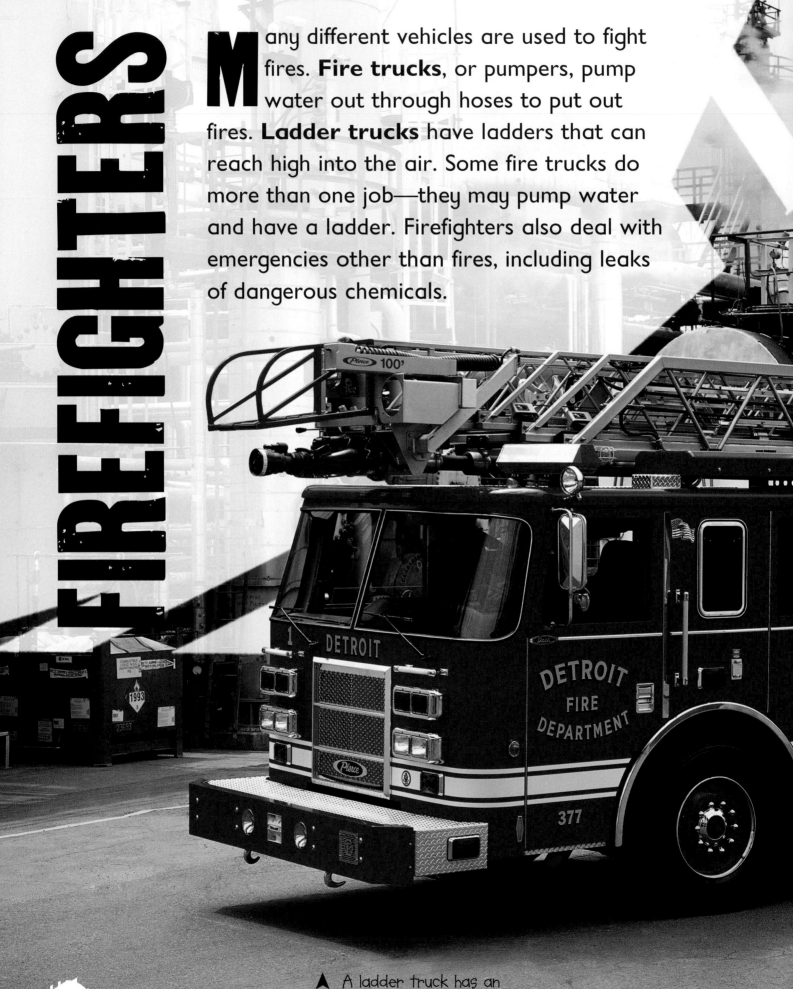

FIREFIGHTERS

Many different vehicles are used to fight fires. **Fire trucks**, or pumpers, pump water out through hoses to put out fires. **Ladder trucks** have ladders that can reach high into the air. Some fire trucks do more than one job—they may pump water and have a ladder. Firefighters also deal with emergencies other than fires, including leaks of dangerous chemicals.

▲ A ladder truck has an **extension** ladder on the top.

LADDERS AND PLATFORMS

Ladders and platforms lift firefighters high above the ground. A hose runs the length of the ladder and carries water to nozzles at the top. Ladders and platforms also help firefighters rescue people from tall buildings.

◄ The tallest aerial ladders and platforms can reach more than 100 feet above the ground.

Jaws of Life

In addition to putting out fires, firefighters also rescue people trapped in vehicles after car accidents. They use specially designed tools, called the "Jaws of Life." These can slice through metal and force apart pieces of wreckage.

▲ The "Jaws of Life" cutters used by firefighters can chop off a car's roof in seconds to reach people trapped inside.

221

FIRE CHASER

The first car to go faster than the speed of sound was called the Thrust SSC. It was so fast that a specially designed firefighting vehicle was created to reach the car quickly if it caught fire. It was called the Jaguar XLR "Firechase" car and could reach speeds of 155 mph. Fortunately, it never had to be used.

▼ Jaguar firefighting cars are designed to reach a fire as quickly as possible.

Heat vision

Smoke makes it difficult for firefighters to see each other inside a burning building. They use special cameras, called **thermal cameras**, to find their way around. Thermal cameras make pictures from heat instead of light and can "see" in complete darkness. Through a thermal camera, hot things—such as flames or someone's body—look bright, and cooler things look dark.

◄ This picture of a firefighter was taken by a thermal camera.

Fire trucks

Fire trucks are built to carry a team of firefighters and all the equipment they need to put out a fire. Water from a tank inside the vehicle is pumped out onto the fire through hoses. If more water is needed, it can be taken from underground water pipes. Hoses, tools, and other equipment are carried in lockers. Most fire trucks are red, but in some places you might also see bright green or yellow fire trucks.

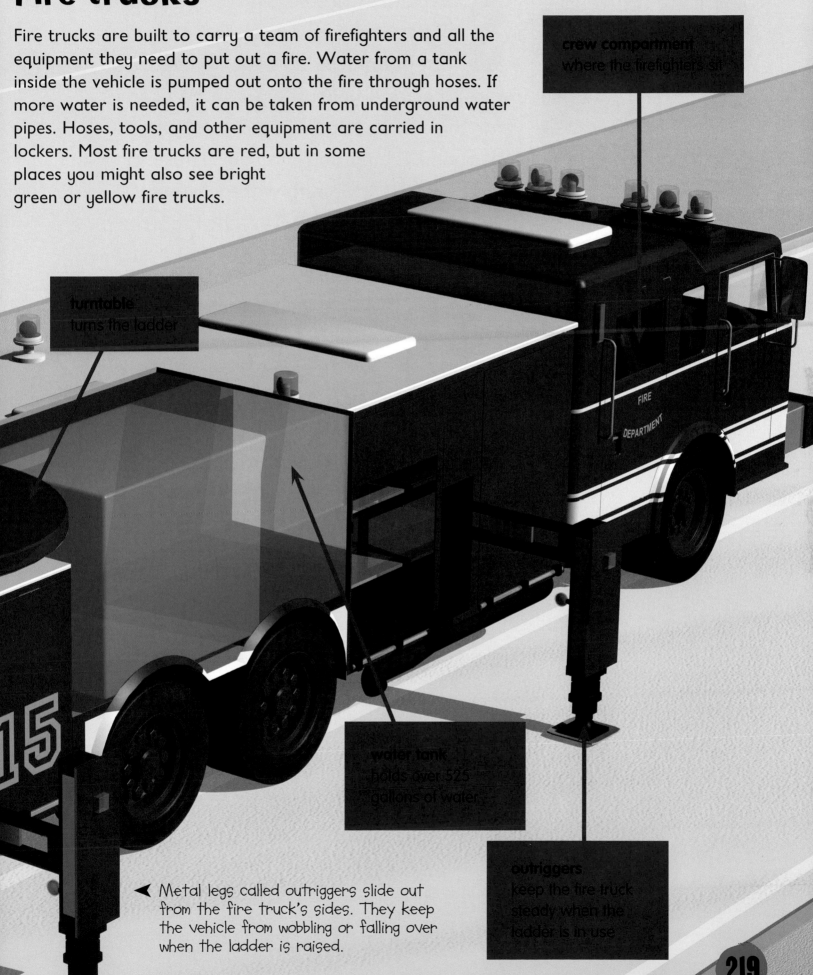

crew compartment
where the firefighters sit

turntable
turns the ladder

water tank
holds over 525 gallons of water

outriggers
keep the fire truck steady when the ladder is in use

◄ Metal legs called outriggers slide out from the fire truck's sides. They keep the vehicle from wobbling or falling over when the ladder is raised.

FIREFIGHTING AIRCRAFT

Some fires are so big—or so difficult for firefighters to get to—that they are fought by aircraft. Ordinary airplanes and helicopters can be used for this work, but there are also specially designed firefighting aircraft. These aircraft fight fires by dropping water, foam, or chemicals onto them. The chemicals are often colored bright red. The color stains the ground so that pilots can see where the chemicals have landed.

Firehawk

The Sikorsky Firehawk is a firefighting helicopter. To take in water, it hovers just above the surface of the water while a special pipe called a snorkel hose is lowered down to suck up water into the tank.

The Sikorsky ➤ Firehawk helicopter can fill its 1,000-gallon water tank in just 60 seconds. It then flies off to drop the water onto large fires.

◄ A Douglas Invader firefighting plane swoops over a fire and drenches it with chemicals.

FLYING BOAT

The Bombardier 415 is specially designed for firefighting. It is a flying boat, so it can land on water as well as fly through the air. It can scoop up more than 1,600 gallons of water in 12 seconds before it takes off again. It then flies over the fire and drops the water on it.

▲ Doors in the bottom of the Bombardier 415 open to drop its cargo of water.

DISASTER HELP

When a flood, earthquake, or hurricane strikes and large numbers of people need help, huge **cargo** planes full of supplies fly to their aid. These giant airplanes usually move equipment for armies or carry goods from country to country. One of the largest of all cargo planes is the Lockheed C-5 Galaxy. The whole nose and tail of this airplane lift up so that supplies can be loaded onto it. In an emergency, cargo planes carry lifesaving supplies to airports near the disaster. From there, smaller airplanes, helicopters, and trucks move the supplies to where they are needed.

Helicopter aid

Helicopters are ideal aircraft for delivering emergency supplies. They can land on a small patch of land, or hover close to the ground and hand out boxes of supplies.

◄ Army helicopters deliver emergency supplies after a natural disaster.

Supplies are loaded ➤ onto a Lockheed C-5 Galaxy on platforms. Rollers in the airplane's floor make it easier to slide heavy loads across it.

AIRPORT FIREFIGHTERS

Every big airport has its own firefighting service that deals with spilled fuel, fires, and crashed aircraft. They also help with medical emergencies. Airport firefighting vehicles are called aircraft rescue and firefighting (ARFF) vehicles. Airport fire trucks are different from other fire trucks because they are specially designed for fighting aircraft fires. Big firefighting vehicles have a nozzle on the roof or front bumper that sprays foam over the fire. Firefighters move a **joystick** to steer the nozzle.

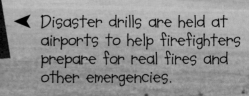

◄ Disaster drills are held at airports to help firefighters prepare for real fires and other emergencies.

Reaching inside

Some airport fire trucks have a folding mechanical arm on top. A pipe carries water or foam to a nozzle at the end. A firefighter uses a joystick to steer the end of the arm inside the door of a burning airplane to soak it with water or foam.

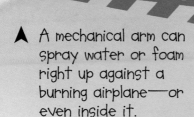

▲ A mechanical arm can spray water or foam right up against a burning airplane—or even inside it.

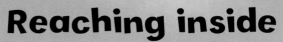

▲ Fires and other emergencies at airports are tackled by a variety of vehicles. These range from small pickup trucks carrying medical supplies and tools to large firefighting machines.

ROBOTS

Robot rescuers can go into places that are too dangerous for people. They search for survivors in collapsed buildings after an **earthquake** or hurricane, and bring water or vital medical help. They also help defuse unexploded bombs. An operator drives the robot. From a safe distance away, the operator sees through the robot's cameras and steers it by moving a small joystick. A variety of tools can be attached to the robot's mechanical arms to do different jobs.

camera

Like tanks, most ➤ emergency and rescue robots have **treads** so they can be driven over rough ground.

treads

228

BOMB DISPOSAL

Making an unexploded bomb safe is a very dangerous job. The people who do it sometimes use robots. A robot is driven up to the bomb. The operator can see the bomb from a safe distance through the robot's cameras. The robot's mechanical arm is fitted with tools or a gun to break windows, open doors, or pull the bomb out.

◄ Robots carry unexploded bombs away to an area where they can be safely exploded.

gripper camera

gripper

Search-and-rescue

Search-and-rescue robots are tiny because they have to be able to get through small spaces in rubble and wreckage. They may look like toys, but they do a very important job.

Search-and-rescue robots ►
are used to find people trapped under rubble when buildings collapse. They have lights and cameras to show their operator what they find.

EMERGENCY ROCKETS

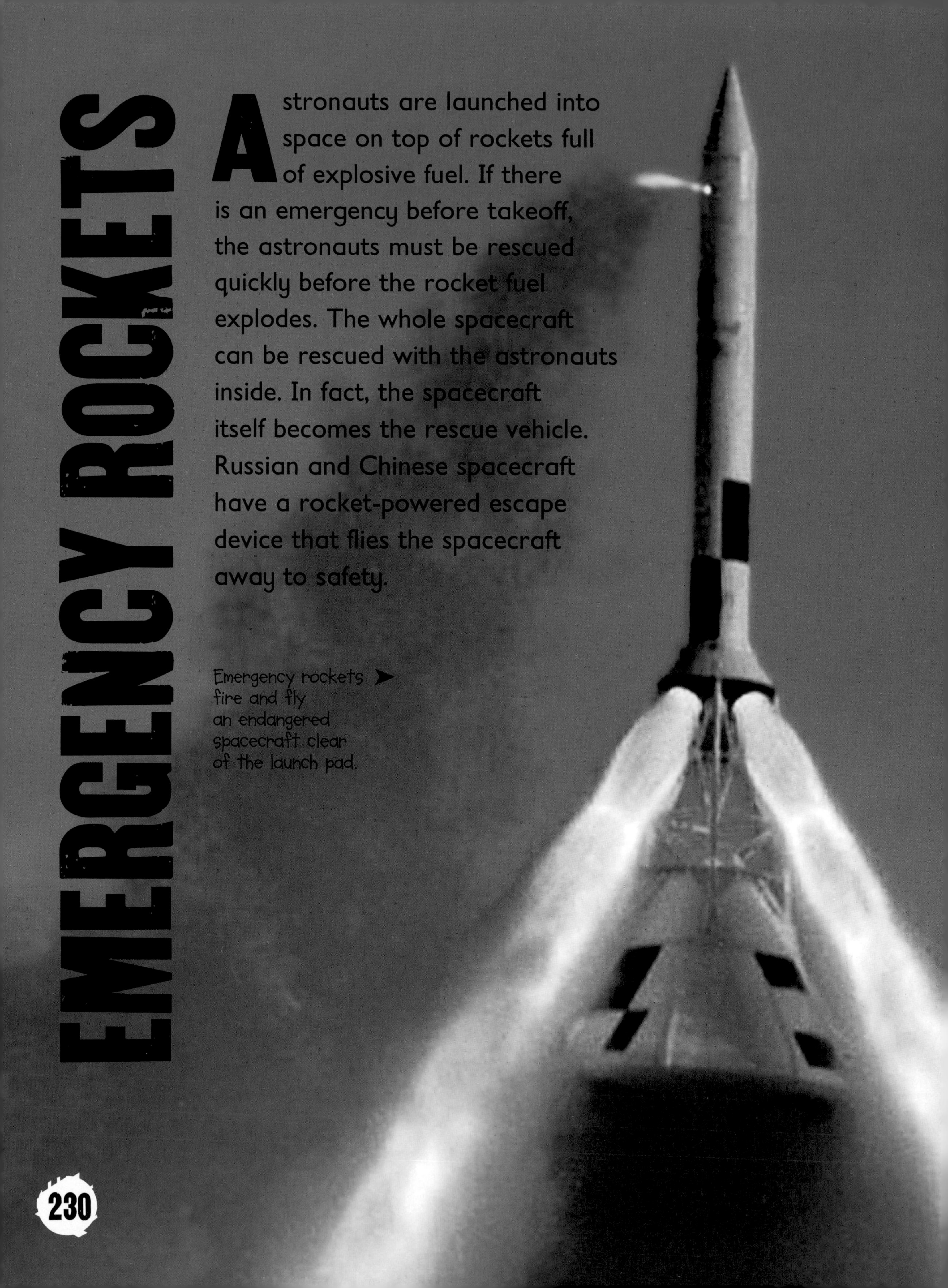

Astronauts are launched into space on top of rockets full of explosive fuel. If there is an emergency before takeoff, the astronauts must be rescued quickly before the rocket fuel explodes. The whole spacecraft can be rescued with the astronauts inside. In fact, the spacecraft itself becomes the rescue vehicle. Russian and Chinese spacecraft have a rocket-powered escape device that flies the spacecraft away to safety.

Emergency rockets ➤
fire and fly
an endangered
spacecraft clear
of the launch pad.

SHUTTLE EMERGENCY

If astronauts have to leave a space shuttle in a hurry while it is still on the ground, they climb into baskets at the top of the launch tower. The baskets slide down wires to the ground. The astronauts then rush inside an earth-covered room called a bunker, where they will be safe.

Space shuttle ➤ astronauts practice an emergency escape by sliding more than 2,000 feet down a wire in a basket.

Armored rescue

If space shuttle astronauts need to be saved in an emergency, rescuers head for the launch pad in armored vehicles. These special vehicles give the rescuers the best protection from fire and explosions. The rescue team may wear special suits to protect them from heat.

◀ Armored cars carry rescuers to the space shuttle launch pad in an emergency.

231

aerial platform a type of firefighting vehicle with a long arm called a boom that can be raised high into the air; at the end of the boom is a bucket or platform, in which one or two firefighters can stand

aerobatics stunt flying by pilots competing against each other or flying together in an air display

aerodynamic made in the best shape for moving through air as fast as possible

air ambulance an aircraft for carrying sick or injured people

air current a moving flow of air

airliner an aircraft used by an airline to fly fare-paying passengers

air pollution harmful substances in the air; burning oil or gasoline in vehicle engines produces harmful substances that spread through the air

air resistance the slowing effect of air when something tries to move through it; streamlined shapes cause the least air resistance

airship a powered aircraft full of a lighter-than-air gas, such as helium

all-terrain vehicle (ATV) a small vehicle like a motorcycle, but with four wheels; ATVs are sometimes used for getting around farms or helping to round up animals

arrester cable a length of wire stretched across the deck of an aircraft carrier to catch the tail hooks of aircraft as they land

artificial something that is man-made and not found naturally

asphalt a black substance that is used to make road surfaces

asteroid a space object made of rock, smaller than a planet, that orbits the Sun

astronaut someone who travels into space

astronomer a scientist who studies the stars, planets, and other objects in space

atmosphere the air that surrounds the Earth, or the gases that surround other planets or moons

attachment a piece of machinery that can be fitted to another machine; a plow is an attachment that can be fitted to a tractor

auger a screw-shaped tool that can drill holes into the ground

backhoe a digging machine with a mechanical arm that has a bucket on the end

bale a bundle of hay, straw, cotton, or other plant material

baling machine a machine that collects hay or straw together into large bundles, or bales

barge a flat-bottomed boat for carrying cargo

bathyscaphe a type of craft that can be submerged and used for deep-sea exploration

beam a long, narrow piece of wood, metal, or concrete, often supported at both ends

billion one thousand million

blacktop like asphalt, a black substance that is used to make road surfaces

blade part of a racing bike's wheels, connecting the center of the wheel to the rim; unlike spokes, they look thin from the front and wide from the side, like a knife blade

blended wing body (BWB) a new type of airliner that is one big wing with no separate body or tail

boom the long arm on a crane

booster a rocket that provides extra power to help a bigger rocket take off

bow the front end of a boat or ship

bridge the part of a ship raised high above the deck; the captain commands the ship from the bridge

bucket the part of a digging machine that scoops up dirt

bucket wheel excavator a large digging machine with a huge wheel at the front, to which lots of buckets are attached; as the wheel turns, the buckets dig up dirt

bulk carrier a type of cargo ship that carries raw materials such as coal

bulldozer a powerful machine with a large blade at the front that can push huge amounts of dirt

Bullet Train a nickname for the Shinkansen high-speed train in Japan; it was given this name because of the shape and speed of the first models in the 1960s

business jet an aircraft used to provide air taxi and private flight services to businesses and individuals

cab the part of a locomotive or train where the driver sits

car a railway carriage for passengers

carbon fiber a strong material made from threads of carbon that have been heated and stretched

cargo goods and materials carried by an aircraft, ship, or truck; also called freight

catamaran a boat with two hulls

catapult   a device that can hurl an object into the air; catapults are used on warships to launch airplanes into the air

cockpit   the part of a plane where the pilot sits and flies the plane; also the part of a racing car where the driver sits

combine   a farm machine that cuts crops such as wheat or barley and separates the grain (seeds) from the stalks

comet   a ball of rock, dust, and ice in orbit around the Sun

commercial   run as a business

communicate   to pass on or share information

commuter   a person who travels the same route to work every day, often by train or car; commuters usually travel several miles from where they live into the towns or cities where they work

compactor   a heavy vehicle driven across soft dirt to squash it down and make it harder

concrete mixer truck   a truck that has a large, round container on its back in which concrete is mixed

container ship   a ship designed to carry containers full of goods

control systems   parts of a plane that make sections of the wings and tail move in order to steer the plane

conveyor belt   a moving belt that is used to move goods or materials from place to place

countdown   the time, counted backward to zero, leading to the launch of a rocket

crawler-transporters   giant vehicles used at the Kennedy Space Center in Florida for carrying space shuttles from the place where they are built to the launch pad

cruiser   a high-speed warship

cruise ship   a large ship that carries its passengers to many different destinations

cultivator   a farm machine that stirs up the top layer of soil

cutting head   a part of a machine with sharp wheels or teeth for digging through the ground

cylinder   a tube-shaped part of an engine where the fuel is burned

deck   a floor with passenger compartments in a train or ship

demolish   to pull down or destroy

destroyer   a small, heavily armed warship that travels at high speed

diesel engine   a type of engine in some cars, buses, and trucks that burns an oil called diesel oil

diesel oil   a type of oil burned inside a diesel engine

disc   something that is circular in shape; metal discs are found on harrows and are used to cut through the soil

ditch   a long, narrow passage dug in the ground to help water drain away

diving bell   a metal tank with an opening at the bottom; diving bells are lowered into the sea to rescue people trapped in submarines

dock   to link up with a spacecraft; spacecraft dock by locking themselves together

docking port   the part on a spacecraft where another craft can lock onto it; hatches (doors) in the ports open after docking to let astronauts go through

downforce   the downward pressure on a racing car caused by the shape of the car and its wings; downforce helps the car's tires grip the ground and go around bends faster without skidding

drag bike   a racing bike that takes part in drag races

dragster   a drag racing car or bike

drag strip   a straight racing track about 1,312 feet long where dragsters race two at a time

dump truck   a truck with a large open container called a box on the back, which is emptied by tipping it up

earthquake   a violent shaking of the ground caused by movements in the Earth's crust

environment   the natural world

equator   an imaginary line around the Earth midway between the North and South Poles

EVA   extravehicular activity, another name for a spacewalk

excavator   a machine with a bucket that can dig up large amounts of soil or other materials

expand   to become bigger

experimental   for testing; an experimental plane is built specially to test something, for example, a new type of engine or wing

extension   lengthening or enlarging

fairing   a streamlined cover fitted around part of a motorcycle to reduce air resistance

famine   a shortage of food in a country, which means that people have very little or nothing to eat

ferry   a ship that makes short trips between sea ports

fertilizer   a mixture that is added to soil to feed plants

fire truck   a firefighting vehicle that pumps water out through hoses onto a fire; also called a fire engine or pumper

flare stack   a tower on an oil rig through which extra natural gas is released into the air

flight deck   the part of a plane or space shuttle where the pilots sit and control the craft

foil   a "wing" on a boat or ship that lifts it out of the water so that it can travel at high speed

forage harvester   a farm machine that picks up hay or plant stalks; they are then blown out of a chute into a wagon and made into silage

Formula 1   an international motor-racing championship for single-seat cars built according to certain specifications

foundation   the bottom layer of a building; foundations make a strong, even surface on which the rest of a building can be built

four-wheel drive   a car where all four wheels are driven by the engine

freight   goods being transported from one place to another; also called cargo

frigate   a warship that is often used to protect other warships

fuel   a liquid burned inside an engine to power the vehicle

fuel cell   a machine that combines hydrogen and oxygen to make electricity; also another name for a racing car's fuel tank

fumes   smelly or harmful gases

gasoline   a fuel burned inside most car engines; also known as petrol

gas tanker   a ship that carries gas

gears   toothed wheels; car and motorcycle engines are connected to the road wheels by a set of gears; bicycle gears drive a chain, which turns the bike's back wheel; changing gear changes the speed of the car or bike

glider   a plane that flies without engine power by using rising currents of air; gliders are also called sail-planes

gondola   a compartment under an airship for the crew and passengers

grader   a vehicle with a sharp blade underneath; the blade smoothes out bumps on the ground as the grader drives along

gravity   the force that pulls objects toward each other; gravity keeps everything from flying off the planet into space, and it holds the planets in their orbits around the Sun; gravity makes it hard to go uphill and easy to go downhill

greenhouses   buildings made from glass in which crops that need a lot of warmth and sunlight are grown

grooved   a surface that has hollows between raised areas

hammer   an air-driven tool that fits on the end of an excavator's arm instead of a digging bucket; it is used to break up concrete

hangar   a place in which aircraft are stored

harrow   a farm machine pulled by a tractor that uses discs or spikes to break up clumps of soil; harrows are used to flatten the soil

harvesttime   when crops are cut and collected

hay   grass that has been cut and dried

heat shield   part of a spacecraft designed to protect it from the intense heat caused by entering an atmosphere at high speed from space

high-speed train   a train that goes faster than about 125 mph

hoist   a machine that can lift something into the air

hold   a space or compartment in a plane for carrying cargo

horsepower   a measurement of power; the power of a car engine is measured in horsepower

hover   to stay in the same place in the air while flying

hovercraft   a vessel that travels across water or land atop a cushion of air

hull   the part of a boat or ship that sits in the water

hurricane   a huge circular or spiral-shaped storm with winds powerful enough to flatten some buildings; these violent storms are called hurricanes in the Atlantic Ocean and typhoons in the Indian and Pacific Oceans

hydrofoil   a type of boat or ship that travels above the surface of the water

hydrogen   a gas that is lighter than air and burns very easily; cars of the future will probably use it as a fuel

hydroplane   a high-speed racing boat that skims across the surface of the water

IndyCar   a racing car that takes part in Indy Racing in the United States

inflatable   something that can be filled with air; an inflatable boat has a rubber tube around the top that is filled with air; this helps the boat to float

infrared   a type of invisible energy, like light, but made of longer waves that we cannot see; hot objects give out infrared waves

insulation   a material used to keep something at an even temperature

International Space Station   a huge manned spacecraft that orbits the Earth; astronauts can live in the space station for several months or even years

irrigation   a system of watering crops in fields when there is not enough rain

jet engine   a type of aircraft engine that burns fuel to produce a jet of hot gas; the force of the jet pushes the plane through the air

joystick   a handle found in a vehicle, and which is used to control the movements of the vehicle or its equipment

Jumbo Jet   the nickname for the Boeing 747 airliner, because of its huge size

kit   a set of parts to make something

ladder truck   a firefighting vehicle that has a ladder

lander   a spacecraft, or part of a spacecraft, that lands on another planet or moon

launch   to use extra power to send off a vehicle or rocket very fast

launch pad   the platform from which a rocket takes off

levitation   rising up into the air

lifeboat   a boat specially built for rescuing people at sea

liner   a large passenger ship that transports people on long-distance trips across the ocean

liter   a space equal in size to 61 cubic inches (1,000 cc, or cubic centimeters); the size of the cylinders inside an engine, where the fuel burns, is measured in liters, cc, or cubic inches

loader   a machine with a big bucket at the front that can scoop up materials and load them into a truck

locomotive   an engine that moves under its own power and pulls passenger carriages or freight wagons

magnetism   the ability of a magnet to pull iron toward it

maiden flight   a plane's first flight

maneuverable   able to be steered easily and quickly

manure   animal waste, which is often spread onto the land as a natural material to feed plants

mass-produced   built in large numbers

mass transit   a railway for moving a large number of people across a city quickly

mast   a tall pole on a ship or a boat that holds up sails or rigging

mechanical   something that is worked by a machine

mechanical arm   a metal arm that is worked by a machine

metro   an underground railway beneath a city

microlight   a small, simple and inexpensive aircraft; microlights are called ultralights or light-sport aircraft in some countries

milk tank truck   a truck with a large container in which milk is transported from dairy farms

mine trucks   large trucks that dig up and carry materials from mines

miniature   much smaller than normal

missile   a weapon that is launched at a target

mobile crane   a crane with wheels that can travel by road

module   a section or compartment of a spacecraft that can be detached from the rest of the spacecraft

monorail   a track with a single rail for a vehicle to move along

moon   a natural satellite orbiting a planet

mower   a machine that cuts grass

NASA   the U.S. National Aeronautics and Space Administration, the organization in charge of American spaceflights

nebula   a vast cloud of dust or gas in space

network   railway tracks connected to each other, linking places

nimble   able to move and turn quickly and easily

nitrogen   a gas; most of the air around us is made of nitrogen

nozzle   a narrow metal tube through which fire engines and fire boats pump water onto fires; a nozzle may be attached to the vehicle, or it may be attached to the end of a hose

nuclear-powered warship   a warship powered by nuclear energy

nutrients   vitamins and minerals that keep plants and animals healthy

off-road truck   a truck that works on rough ground; some off-road trucks never travel on roads

orbit   to circle something

organic   something grown without the use of artificial chemicals

outriggers   strong metal legs that reach out from the side of a machine or a vehicle to give it a wider base and so make it steadier

oxen   male cattle

parachute   a large sheet of light fabric attached to a harness worn by a person; the fabric opens out as the person falls through the air and slows him or her down to a safe speed for landing

paraglider   a wing-shaped parachute

paramedic   a person who provides emergency medical care

paramotor   a motor and propeller worn by a pilot hanging from a paraglider; paramotor gliders are also called powered parachutes and powered paragliders

patrol   to move around a place to watch what is happening there

paver   a machine that lays a new road surface

payload bay   the part of the space shuttle orbiter where cargo is carried

pendulum   a weight swinging from side to side on a wire or rod

piles   long metal or concrete pillars that are sunk into the ground to provide supports on which a building can be constructed

piston   a drum-shaped part of an engine that fits inside a cylinder; the piston can slide in and out of the cylinder; burning fuel in the cylinder pushes the piston out of the cylinder

plow   a farm machine pulled by a tractor to turn over the top of the soil

pneumatic drill   a powerful drill operated by compressed air

pole   the farthest point either north (North Pole) or south (South Pole) of the Earth's equator

pollute   to add unwanted or harmful substances to the environment

post driver   a machine that is used to knock posts firmly into the ground

post hole auger   a machine that is used to cut round holes into the ground, into which fence posts can be placed

power the speed at which energy changes from one form to another form; a more powerful car engine changes fuel energy into movement faster than a less powerful engine

powerboat a high-speed boat that is driven forward by a powerful engine

power cables lengths of wire that carry electricity to a building

power car another name for the locomotive, or pulling vehicle, of an electric train

power takeoff (PTO) part of a farm tractor that supplies engine power to another machine

prong a long, narrow, pointed part of a tool or machine

propeller a part of an airplane that moves the plane through the air by spinning long, thin blades in front of the engine; also a part of a ship or boat that moves it through the water; a spinning propeller spins and pushes against the water, thrusting the vessel in the opposite direction

pulverizer a machine that crushes something completely

radar a way of finding distant aircraft by sending out radio waves and picking up any reflections that bounce back from the aircraft; also, equipment used by police officers to check the speed of vehicles

rake a piece of equipment with a number of sharp points; pulling a rake across the ground sweeps up mown grass or plant stalks; farm rakes are pulled by tractors

rally a type of race for cars that set off one at a time; the drivers try to set the fastest time; a rally is usually divided into a series of separate timed events called stages

rapid transit a railway for moving people across a city quickly

receiver a radio that takes in, or receives, radio signals

reentry coming back into the Earth's atmosphere from space

remote far away from populated areas

restore to bring back into good condition

rigid something that does not bend

road header a machine that makes tunnels by grinding through rock

rocket a type of engine with its own supply of fuel and the oxygen needed to burn the fuel; rockets are extremely powerful, unlike gas engines, and are also able to work in space where there is no air

roller a machine that flattens and hardens the surface of a newly laid road

roller coaster a raised railway, usually found at a theme park, with curves and steep climbs; people ride in open cars for fun and excitement

roll-on, roll-off a ship designed so that cars can drive straight onto or off it

rotor blades the metal blades found on a helicopter that turn to make it take off

ROV remotely operated vehicle—a machine controlled from a safe distance by an operator; ROVs are used for dangerous jobs, such as making bombs safe

SAFER backpack a backpack worn by space shuttle and International Space Station astronauts when they work outside their spacecraft; if an astronaut drifts away from the spacecraft, he or she can fire jets of gas from the backpack to fly back to safety

satellite a smaller object orbiting a larger one; communications satellites orbit the Earth; they can pick up signals from one place and send them to a different part of the world

scramjet a new type of jet engine for very fast aircraft that can fly at more than five times the speed of sound

scraper a machine that moves earth by scraping it up into a big box called a hopper

seedling a very young plant

service train the railway train that follows a tunnel boring machine and provides it with power

sewer a system of pipes to take waste water away from houses and buildings

silage animal food that is made from green plants

single-seater a car with only one seat

siren a piece of equipment that sends out a loud wailing noise

skid steer loader a small digging machine that steers by stopping the wheels or tracks on one side

solar car a car powered by sunlight

solar cell a device that changes sunlight into electricity; a sheet of solar cells is also called a solar panel

solar panel part of a satellite or space probe that makes electricity from sunlight using solar cells

solar power powered by the Sun; solar-powered cars change sunlight into electricity to power a motor

solar-powered a device that uses solar power

solar system the Sun and all the planets, moons, comets, asteroids, dust, and gas that orbit it

solid rocket booster a rocket that burns solid fuel to give a bigger rocket or space vehicle extra power for takeoff

sonar a way of using sound waves to find objects underwater; if an object is found, the sound waves "bounce" off it to show where it is

space plane a rocket-powered aircraft with wings that can soar into space and land again on Earth like an airliner

space probe an unmanned spacecraft that explores space and sends information back to Earth

space shuttle a rocket-powered space vehicle that can travel into space multiple times

space station a large spacecraft that stays in space for months or years and is run by a series of crews

speed of sound the speed at which sound travels through a substance; the speed of sound in air depends on the temperature: on a cool day, the speed of sound in air is about 760 mph

spoke one of the many thin pieces of metal that connect the center of a wheel to the rim

sports car a small, lightweight, nimble, fast car that's fun to drive

Sputnik I the first satellite ever launched from Earth, in 1957; Sputnik is a Russian word meaning "traveling companion"

stage part of a rocket with its own engine and fuel; when one stage has used up all of its fuel, it falls away and the next stage takes over; also, one of the timed race events that forms part of a car rally

star an object in the sky that is far bigger than any planet; stars give out light and heat

stern the back end of a boat or ship

streamlined smooth and gently curving; a streamlined object moves through air easily and quickly without producing a lot of air resistance

streamliner a high-speed motorcycle with a slim, smooth, gently curving body around the whole bike and its rider; streamliners are used to set speed records

streetcar a passenger vehicle running on rails along city streets

stunt an unusual, difficult, and sometimes spectacular act; stunt flying is also called aerobatics

submarine a large craft that can dive underwater for days, weeks, or even months and come back to the surface again

submerge to dive below the surface of the water

submersible a small craft that can dive into deep water for short periods of time

subway an underground railway

supercar a very expensive high-performance car

supersonic faster than the speed of sound

swather a farm machine that cuts crops and bundles them into windrows

telehandler a farm vehicle with an extending boom, or arm, for lifting heavy loads such as hay bales

telescope an instrument for studying distant objects

thermal camera a camera that makes pictures from heat instead of light; also called an infrared camera or a thermal imaging system

threshing separating the seeds of a crop such as wheat from the rest of the plant

thrust the force produced by a rocket engine

tide the rise and fall of the sea level

tower crane a crane that sits on top of a tall metal tower

tractor a farm vehicle used for pulling trailers and machines

tractor-trailer a large truck that can bend in the middle

trailer a container with four wheels that is attached to a tractor and pulled behind it

tram a passenger vehicle running on rails along city streets

transplanter a machine that puts small plants in the ground, one by one

transponder short for transmitter-responder, a piece of equipment that sends out a coded radio signal to identify a vehicle; planes and trains carry transponders

tread a belt made from metal sections linked together; tracked vehicles, like tanks, have a track on each side around its wheels

trench a long, narrow cut in the ground

trimaran a lightweight sailboat that has three hulls

tugboat a small but very powerful boat that tows or pushes bigger ships

tunnel boring machine (TBM) a machine designed to cut its way through the earth to create a tunnel

udder the part of a cow in which milk is made

ultra truck any of the world's biggest trucks; ultra trucks are used in the mining industry

universe everything that exists, including the Earth, stars, and planets

V-8 a type of car engine with eight cylinders

vertical straight upward

vessel a machine that travels on water

video equipment fitted to some police cars and police motorcycles for recording the view ahead

volt a measurement of electricity

wagon a railcar for carrying freight

wakeboarder someone who skis behind a motorboat on a single board

waterjet a type of engine that works by shooting water out of the back of a ship to push it forward

welded joined by melting together; two pieces of metal are welded by heating them until they melt, run together, and set hard again

winch a machine used to lift or pull heavy objects

windrow a long, low ridge or row of hay

wing part of a plane with a special shape that lifts the plane upward when it moves through the air

X-planes a series of experimental aircraft built in the United States to test new ideas for future aircraft